June 16, 1974

Happy Father's Day

to Grandpa B.

from Jennifer
Janet &
Jean

THE ANSWER BOOK OF
SPORTS

Answers to Hundreds of Questions about the World of Sports

By BILL MAZER

GROSSET & DUNLAP • Publishers • NEW YORK

FOREWORD

There has already been so much said about how sports provides a common meeting ground for people of all ages that I'm not about to add even a word.

What I would like to say as a foreword is that my first literary effort was dedicated to my wife who, as I put it then, "allowed me the time to pursue my labor of love with limitless time."

This work belongs strictly to those wonderful young people who helped me fill air time on radio station WNBC in New York for four and a half years with their questions and answers. It may sound as corny as "thanks to those who made this possible." I'll risk that, because at least I know how true and with what amount of feeling the expression is made.

So here is another session of questions and answers done in the same spirit as that produced in my meetings with sports fans everywhere.

Please enjoy.

Bill Mazer

PICTURE CREDITS

Key to picture position: t-top; b-bottom; l-left; r-right; c-center. Combinations: br-bottom right, etc.

United Press International, Inc.: 11 l, 13 b, 17 c, 57 l, 59, 61, 62, 64 r.

Wide World Photos: 14 r, 16, 17 1, 21, 22, 25 r, 26, 27, 28, 31, 33, 35, 37, 38, 39, 40, 41, 42, 44, 45, 47, 48, 50, 53, 71, 73, 75, 76, 78, 79, 80, 82, 84, 85, 86, 89, 92, 95, 97, 100, 102, 105, 111, 113, 115, 117, 118, 121, 122, 125, 127, 128, 129, 130, 132, 133, 134, 135, 136, 137, 138, 140, 141, 142, 145, 147, 149, 151, 152, 153, 155.

1973 PRINTING

Library of Congress Catalog Card Number: 72-86698

ISBN: 0-448-04475-7 (TRADE EDITION) ISBN: 0-448-03328-3 (LIBRARY EDITION)

Copyright © 1969, by Bill Mazer

CONTENTS

Page

BASEBALL 5

Who invented baseball? 5

Who deserves the credit as the creator of modern baseball? 7

How do you score a baseball game? 8

Who is baseball's all-time greatest ball player? 9

Who was baseball's last .400 hitter? 10

What is considered baseball's greatest record? 10

Who are the nine players who have won the triple crown of batting? 10

How many players have hit four home runs in a single game? 12

What team has won the most pennants in baseball? 13

What players got three thousand or more hits in their lifetime? 14

Who holds the record for most-runs-batted-in a season? 15

Who holds the record for most stolen bases in a season? 15

Have two men on the same team hit 50 home runs in the same season? 16

How many pitchers have won more than three hundred games? 17

How many pitchers have hurled no-hitters in both leagues? 17

How is a pitcher's ERA rated? 19

Who struck out the most men in a lifetime? 20

What pitcher broke a record in 1968 that had lasted for 55 years? 21

What is considered the greatest game ever pitched? 22

Who almost pitched a no-hitter in a World Series? 23

Has only one left-hander won three games in a World Series? 24

Did Babe Ruth ever pitch in a World Series? 24

Which pitcher holds the record for most strike-outs in a World Series game? 25

What was Bobby Thomson's "shot heard round the world"? 26

Who inaugurated the All-Star Game? 28

FOOTBALL 31

Who invented football? 31

What is the single-wing? 32

Page

What is the basic "T" formation? 33

What is the winged "T"? 33

What is the pro "T"? 34

What is an odd defense? What is an even defense? 34

What is a zone defense? What is a man for man? 35

What is a blitz? 35

What is an eligible receiver? 36

When was the forward pass first introduced to football? 36

Is O. J. Simpson the greatest runner of them all? 37

Who was "Wrong Way" Riegels? 39

How did the "Four Horsemen" term originate? 40

Who were Mr. Inside and Mr. Outside? 41

Who once made four long touch-down runs in the first ten minutes? 41

Who did they call "Bronko"? 43

What football player became a Justice of the U.S. Supreme Court? 43

Who was the greatest all-around player? 45

But how about the ones who play today? 46

Where and when was the first pro football game played? 51

Which two teams played the longest pro championship game? 52

BASKETBALL 53

How did the dribble come into being? 54

Has any college team won the NCAA Championship three consecutive years? 56

Who was basketball's first big man? 58

Who influenced defense more than any other player? 59

Who is "Wilt the Stilt"? 60

Who is the best all-around player? 62

What is the greatest scoring combination in the history of pro basketball? 63

Which player started the basketball scoring revolution? 65

Who were the original Celtics? 66

Who started the Harlem Globetrotters? 67

Which team holds the longest scholastic winning streak? 68

Page

What is meant by a combination man-for-man zone? 68

What is the all-court press? 69

What are offensive formations? 70

BOXING 71

Who beat John L. Sullivan? 74

Who was known as the Boilermaker? 74

Who finally defeated Jack Johnson? 76

Who was the "Manassa Mauler"? 77

Which fighter scored the most one-round knockouts in title fights? 77

How many heavyweight champions retired undefeated? 78

Where does Muhammed Ali fit in? 81

Who were outstanding in the other divisions? 81

What is the record for most knockdowns in one round? 85

What is the record for most knockdowns in a fight? 86

Which fighter holds the record for most knockouts? 86

What was the longest glove fight on record? 87

How are fights scored? 87

What was the largest live gate in boxing history? 88

What was the largest live attendance at a fight? 88

How many fighters have never been defeated in a pro career? 88

Who refereed the most title bouts? 88

Who was the youngest fighter to win a heavyweight title? 88

HOCKEY 89

Which was the first hockey league? 90

Which came first, the National Hockey League or the Stanley Cup? 90

Which were the first teams in the N.H.L.? 91

Which was the first United States team? 91

What is so special about June 5, 1967? 91

What is the Hart Memorial Trophy? 92

	Page
What is the Clarence S. Campbell award?	93
What is the Prince of Wales Trophy?	93
What is the Art Ross Trophy?	93
What other scoring record fell in 1968-69?	94
What is the Calder Trophy?	96
What is the James Norris Memorial Trophy?	96
What is the Vezina Trophy?	97
Which team has won the Prince of Wales Trophy most?	98
What is the Lady Byng Trophy?	98
What is the Conn Smythe Trophy?	99
Who is hockey's greatest player?	99
Who was the most exciting hockey player?	100
What is unusual about Bill Chadwick?	103
What was the origin of hockey in the United States?	103
Can U.S. teams become National Hockey League players?	104

GOLF | 105 |

When did the British Open start?	106
When did the U.S. Open start?	107
When was the United States Golf Association formed?	107
When was the first amateur championship played?	107
When did the ladies start their championship?	108
Who was Willie Anderson?	108
Who were Vardon and Ray?	108
What young American beat Vardon and Ray?	109
What about the other twenty-year-old, Walter Hagen?	111
What of Hagen's great match with Bobby Jones?	112
How great was Bobby Jones?	112
What is Bobby Jones most famous for?	114
Which player won the U.S. Open by playing the last 28 holes in 100 strokes?	115
How great was Byron Nelson?	116
What about Ben Hogan?	116
What is considered Hogan's greatest feat?	118
What great player has never won the U.S. Open?	119
Who is golf's biggest money maker?	120

	Page
How about the U.S. Open in 1960?	121
Who do they call the "Golden Bear"?	122
What was special about his winning the U.S. Open?	123
Why hasn't Nicklaus won the crowds over?	123
Who are some of these players?	124
What players have won professional golf's Grand Slam?	124
What is the longest hole in one ever made?	124
What about the lady golfers?	125
Who was golf's best known lady player?	126
Who was Joyce Wethered?	126

TRACK AND FIELD | 127 |

What is considered the greatest Olympic feat?	128
What other memorable moments occurred in the 1968 Olympics?	128
Who turned in the greatest one-day performance in track history?	129
Who were the only two men ever to beat Bob Hayes?	130
What great hurdler was also an Olympic 100-meter champion?	131
Who was the short high hurdler who won the 1964 Olympic gold medal in his event?	131
How many Kansans have held world records in the middle distances?	131
Who has run more under-four-minutes miles than anyone else?	132
How important is a big "kick" to a miler?	132
How many men have held seven or more world records at one time?	134
Which four American runners have held world records at two miles or over?	134
Which two pole vaulters cleared 15 feet on the same day?	135
How much extra height does the fiberglass pole provide?	136
Why was Yuri Stepanov's high-jump record called into question?	136
What were John Thomas' and Valery Brumel's highest jumps?	137
In what year did Parry O'Brien retire from the shot put?	138
Who held the shot-put record between 1960 and 1965?	139
What are the ten events of the decathlon?	139

	Page
Who was the only man to defeat Rafer Johnson?	139
Who was America's greatest woman athlete?	140
Who was the woman track star who held seven world records at once?	140

TENNIS | 141 |

When was the game introduced to the United States?	141
Who is considered the greatest player of all time?	142
How many players have won Tennis' Grand Slam?	143
When did open tennis begin?	143
How did the Davis Cup originate?	144
Which nation has won the Davis Cup most times?	144
Who is considered the most successful Davis Cup coach in history?	144
Who won the first American Open?	145
Who was the most dominant figure in U.S. women's tennis?	145
What was the golden era of tennis?	146
Why are some players better on a grass court and others better on a clay court?	146
What was the biggest crowd ever to see a Davis Cup tennis match?	147
Are there any small tennis players who have become great champions?	147
What has been the major change in tennis since the days of Tilden and Budge?	148
What is the Wightman Cup?	148
How many great players have two-handed shots?	148
Who was the player who rose to fame despite having diabetes?	149
What is VASSS?	150
Why has Australia become such a dominant tennis nation?	150
Do top singles players make good doubles players?	151
What is the outstanding brother-sister act in tennis today?	152
What is the Federation Cup?	152
Who is rated the greatest woman player?	153
Who are some of the other great men players?	154

INDEX | 156 |

Baseball

Abner Doubleday (1819-1893)

Who invented baseball?

Do you know what the toughest question about baseball is? It's: "How was the game invented?"

There's no one answer—because nobody knows for sure!

In 1907 a special committee of officials was named to determine the origin of baseball—that is, to find out who the founder was and where the first game was played. After their "investigation," they decided that Abner Doubleday had laid out the first field and organized the first baseball game in Cooperstown, New York, sometime in 1839. For that reason Cooperstown was selected as the site for the Hall of Fame and Baseball Museum, which were opened in 1939—on the supposed 100th anniversary of baseball.

But that 1907 committee couldn't have been more off base. Later historians discovered that at the time Doubleday was thought to be inventing baseball in Cooperstown he was a cadet at West Point. Furthermore, there was doubt that he had ever even played the game!

So how did baseball start in our country? The best-informed opinion of the historians is that the sport evolved early in the 1800's from cricket

The first league game in baseball was played between teams from New York and Boston on April 29, 1886. As shown in this illustration, the fielders did not wear gloves.

and another English game, rounders, which used posts for bases and had a batter who punched the ball and was put out by being hit with the ball. There were variations of the game known as "Town Ball" and "New York Game."

Some of this confusion about the history of baseball—and the different kinds of baseball—is understandable. What American boy has grown up without playing some variation of baseball? Maybe it was stickball on a city street, where hitting a rubber ball the length of three manhole covers with a broom handle was a homer. Or maybe it was o'cat (one old cat) on an empty lot, with four players on a side and one base. Or softball, played with a softer ball than the one in use now, the kind that had an outside stitch. Softball was popular in my time because you didn't need gloves (equipment was scarce in the depression days). When you had gloves, then you played "hard ball," as we called regular baseball. Now there are the well-organized, well-equipped Little Leagues, Babe Ruth Leagues, American Legion Leagues, etc., but I'll bet we had just as much fun in our pick-up games, without uniforms and adult supervision.

But getting back to history. While the name baseball began to be commonly used as early as the 1820's, there was still no standard form of the game until 1846. On this event historians are in complete accord.

Who deserves the credit as the creator of modern baseball?

He was a young surveyor by the name of Alexander Cartwright. A Knickerbocker Baseball Club was formed that year and Cartwright, a member, was given the job of laying out a diamond and devising the rules of play. Cartwright placed the bases ninety feet apart, set up the foul lines, settled on nine players to a team and three outs to an inning—and even three strikes to a batter! A rule was added that a base runner also could not be put out by throwing the ball at him.

The first game was played at Hoboken, New Jersey, on June 19, 1846, between the Knickerbockers and a team called the New York Nine. Cartwright was the umpire and, ironically, his team was trounced, 23-1!

Cartwright's involvement with baseball ended shortly afterward, but he had done his work well. His original contributions to the game were officially recognized when he was elected to the Hall of Fame.

Cartwright laid down the basic principles, but it took half a century —until nearly 1900—before baseball was played the way we know it today. Pitchers at first were allowed only to throw underhand (the pitcher's box was 46 feet from home plate then), then side-arm, then shoulder-high and finally, in 1884, overhand. The pitching distance was increased, too, until the present 60 feet 6 inches was established in 1893. And it wasn't until 1887 that a batter no longer could call for a high or low pitch! And at one time nine balls were needed to walk a batter, the number gradually decreasing until the four-ball rule was put in effect in 1889.

Alexander Cartwright

7

In the 1890's the custom of the umpire raising his right arm for a strike started.

Bill ("Dummy") Hoy, an outstanding outfielder who played for St. Louis, Cincinnati and Washington from 1888 to 1902, was a deaf mute. Since he couldn't hear the umpire's call when he was batting, the umpires began the arm gestures to tell him what the count was. The custom has prevailed.

As any player can tell you, the official scorer is an important man. He's the sole judge on hits and errors—and think of the many close plays that come up through a season! His decision can mean the difference between a no-hitter and a one-hitter! The scorer's rulings affect batting averages, fielding averages and earned-run averages, and these are the figures on which players negotiate next year's contract. In short, the scorer's decisions can touch a player in his most sensitive area—the pocketbook.

Every fan in the park looks to the scoreboard after one of those borderline hit-or-error cases to see which sign is flashed. But few fans know who the official scorer is and how he is chosen.

How do you score a baseball game?

Scoring a game is much like taking shorthand. There are probably many individual additions, but basically all scorers use the following system: the pitcher is listed as number one; the catcher, number two; the first baseman, three; the second baseman, four; the third baseman, five; the shortstop, six; the leftfielder, seven; the centerfielder, eight; and the rightfielder, nine.

Indicating base hits is very individualized. Some scorers use dashes. I have always indicated them in this fashion: a single would be 1B; a double, 2B; a triple, 3B; a home run, HR. All scorers use the letter "K" to indicate a strike-out and "BB" for a base on balls.

Tell you what—let's make up an inning of play and see what it looks like on the scorecard we have provided.

FIELDING			No.	NAME	Pos.	INNINGS												BATTING											
PO	A	E				1	2	3	4	5	6	7	8	9	10	11	12	AB	R	H	2B	3B	HR	RBI	SO	BB	SH	SB	HP
				BOSWELL	2b																								
				AGEE	cf																								
				GARRETT	3b																								
				JONES	lf																								
				SHAMSKY	rf																								
				KRANEPOOL	1b																								
				HARRELSON	ss																								
				GROTE	c																								
				SEAVER	p																								
				Totals		3/3																							

Who is baseball's all-time greatest ball player?

Settling this one would give King Solomon headaches, but it has provided baseball fans with more enjoyable arguments than you can shake a bat at. Ty Cobb is baseball's all-time leading percentage hitter. He posted a career mark of .367 and led the American League in hitting twelve times. His running ability was about on a par with his hitting—sensational. However, he was just an average outfielder defensively. In contrast, Honus Wagner was a great hitter, a great runner and probably the greatest defensive shortstop of all time. Old-timers are almost unanimous in crediting him with being the perfect ballplayer.

One thing Honus didn't do was become an outstanding pitcher. Babe Ruth was that and more. Ruth's pitching ability was good enough to make him one of the best. But his home-run ability was better, so he became an outfielder, and a really good one. He could throw as well as anyone. He could field—even in those days when his waistline left something to be desired. His running, too, though not spectacular, was better than average. And what a hitter! Experts have often said that Ruth could have hit for almost any average he wanted to, but the fans came to see him hit home runs and 714 times he didn't disappoint them.

If you think my vote goes to Babe Ruth, you're right.

Who was baseball's last .400 hitter?

Hall-of-Famer Ted Williams, who has just unretired himself to become a manager, turned the trick in 1941 when he batted .406. It should be noted that he refused to play it safe on the last day of the season. He was hitting .401 and could have sat out a double-header to insure staying above the rare .400 mark. But he insisted on playing and made six hits to raise his average to .406. Bill Terry of the New York Giants was the last National Leaguer to accomplish the feat with a .401 average in 1930.

Other players of note to bat .400 include Ty Cobb, on three occasions; Rogers Hornsby, also three times; Harry Heilmann; Joe Jackson; George Sisler (twice) and Napoleon Lajoie. These men hit over .400 from the year 1900 on. There were others who hit over .400 prior to 1900.

What is considered baseball's greatest record?

There may be debates in all areas of baseball, but there is almost complete agreement that Joe DiMaggio's 56-game hitting streak is the all-time record. How great it is is apparent when you realize that the best previous consecutive-game hitting record was set before 1900. In 1897, Wee Willie Keeler batted safely in 46 straight games. DiMaggio's hitting streak ended during a night game in Cleveland on July 17, 1941. Starting pitcher Al Smith and relief pitcher Jim Bagby, Jr. get the credit as pitchers of the game, but a third baseman named Ken Keltner made two spectacular plays in the field to "rob" DiMaggio of base hits.

Who are the nine players who have won the triple crown of batting?

Ty Cobb of the Detroit Tigers was the first triple-crown winner in 1909. He hit .377, batted in 115 runs, and topped the league in homers with a grand total of nine. Heinie Zimmerman of the Chicago Cubs was the

Three of baseball's greatest "sluggers": (left) Babe Ruth hitting his sixtieth home run off Tom Zachary in 1927; (center) Ted Williams, formidable "long-ball" hitter of the Boston Red Sox; and (right) Bill Terry, last National Leaguer to bat over .400.

next one in 1912 with 14 homers, 98 RBI's, and an average of .372. Rogers Hornsby twice won the triple crown. He first swept the board in 1922, hitting 42 homers, batting in 152 runs with a .401 average. He repeated in 1925 with 39 homers, 143 RBI's and a .403 average.

After Hornsby's "double," two Philadelphia stars—Jimmy Foxx of the "A's" and Chuck Klein of the Phillies—did it in the same year, 1933. Foxx, batting .356, drove in 163 runs and rapped 48 four-baggers. Klein had 28 homers and 120 runs batted in with a .368 mark.

Lou Gehrig followed the next year with credentials of 49 homers, 165 RBI's and a .363 average.

Joe Medwick of the St. Louis Cardinals did the trick in 1937, getting 31 homers (tying him with Mel Ott of the Giants) and 154 runs batted in with a .374 average.

Ted Williams then did it twice. In 1942 he wrapped up his first triple crown with 36 homers, 137 runs batted in and an average of .356. He won his second in 1947, batting .343 as he stroked 32 four-baggers and drove in 114 runs. He and Hornsby are the only two players who have won batting's triple crown twice.

In 1956, Mickey Mantle of the Yankees had 52 homers, 130 RBI's and a .353 average.

Frank Robinson, playing for the Baltimore Orioles in 1966, hit 49 home runs and drove in 122 runs. His .316 batting average was the best in the league.

The next year Carl Yastrzemski became a triple crowner. His batting average was .326, his RBI's 121, and his home-run total, 44 (tying him with Harmon Killebrew of Minnesota).

How many players have hit four home runs in a single game?

The number is nine. This exclusive list starts back on May 30, 1894, with Robert Lowe of Boston, who remains the only National Leaguer to clout his four in consecutive times at bat.

Ed Delahanty of Philadelphia was the next four-in-a-game hitter on July 13, 1896.

Then it took almost 36 years before Lou Gehrig did it on June 3, 1932, against the Athletics, in his first four trips to the plate. Gehrig nearly became the only player to wallop five, but Al Simmons raced deep into left field to haul down his long drive in the ninth inning.

Chuck Klein joined the club on July 10, 1936, although he needed ten innings to do it.

Twelve years later Pat Seerey of the Chicago White Sox performed the deed on July 18, 1948; he needed eleven innings.

Gil Hodges of the Brooklyn Dodgers was next, on August 31, 1950.

Joe Adcock of the Milwaukee Braves rapped his four on July 31, 1954. Rocky Colavito of the Cleveland Indians followed suit on June 10, 1959.

And Willie Mays of the San Francisco Giants was the last player to do it on April 30, 1961.

An interesting sidelight is that Billy Loes was a spectator at the last four four-homers-in-a-game feats, either on the same team as the hitter or on the opposing team!

Joe DiMaggio   Rogers Hornsby   Lou Gehrig

What team has won the most pennants in baseball?

If you said the New York Yankees, you are right. The Bronx Bombers have won 29 pennants. Although they have slumped in recent years, they are far ahead of any team in either league. The next closest team is a National League team, the New York Giants, who won 15 pennants from 1901 to the time they ceased to exist. If you count pre-1900, add two more to the Giant list.

In accumulating the 29 pennants, the Yankees had the services of Miller Huggins for six of of them, Joe McCarthy for eight, Bucky Harris for one, Casey Stengel for ten, Ralph Houk for three and Yogi Berra for one. The Yankees also have won the World Series more times than any other team. In their 29 appearances, they have come out on top twenty times.

The New York Yankees, in 1939, coming out of their dugout before the start of another World Series championship.

What players got three thousand or more hits in their lifetime?

Only eight have turned the trick. Ty Cobb is the only player with over four thousand hits. His total: 4,191. Then, in descending order, Stan Musial, 3,630; Tris Speaker, 3,515; Honus Wagner, 3,430; Eddie Collins, 3,313; Napoleon Lajoie, 3,251; Paul Waner, 3,152; and Adrian (Cap) Anson, 3,081.

Of those still active in the game and with hopes of getting into the three-thousand club, Willie Mays and Henry Aaron are closing in. Mays had 2,812 hits, going into the 1969 season. The younger Aaron, with 2,792 hits, has said that this is one club he "wants in" before he calls it quits.

Hack Wilson, who hit more home runs in one season than any other National Leaguer.

Stan Musial, after smashing five homers in a double-header against the New York Giants on May 3, 1954.

Ty Cobb, pictured near the end of his career in 1928. The "Georgia Peach," as he was called, was considered the most dangerous base runner of all time.

Who holds the record for most-runs-batted-in in a season?

Lewis Robert (Hack) Wilson of the Chicago Cubs. His name may not mean much to this generation, but this roly-poly man drove in an unbelievable 190 runs in 1930. That same year he hit 56 home runs. The only man to approach this record was the immortal Lou Gehrig of the New York Yankees who owns the American League mark of 184 runs batted-in set in 1931. To get a greater appreciation of these statistics, there hasn't been a hitter who has batted in more than 159 runs (other than Wilson) in the history of the National League.

In the American League, Babe Ruth with 170, Gehrig with 174 and 175, and Hank Greenberg with 170 and 183, are the only hitters in that rare company. Lou Gehrig, Jimmy Foxx, and Babe Ruth, incidentally, batted in a hundred runs or more in a season thirteen times. Stan Musial and Willie Mays accomplished this ten times.

Who holds the record for most stolen bases in a season?

If you said Maury Wills, you're wrong...unless, of course you added the record since 1900. Because, believe it or not, someone named Harry Stovey, playing for Philadelphia, of the old American Association in 1888, stole 156 bases; and in 1891, Billy Hamilton, playing for Philadelphia of the National League, swiped 115. Wills's mark of 104 in 162 games is the modern mark. The great Ty Cobb holds the American League record of 96.

When ballplayers are judged, one usually refers to the bat, the arm and the legs. Ty Cobb (the "Georgia Peach") is the all-time record holder in two categories. His .367 lifetime batting average seems as safe from being overtaken as his mark of 892 stolen bases. The Georgian was truly a peach.

By the way, if anyone asks you what the record is for most stolen bases in a game, the answer (post-1900) is six—accomplished by Eddie Collins of Philadelphia (American League). A former Dodger, Pete Reiser, set a unique record when he stole home seven times in 1946.

The "M&M" boys, Mickey Mantle (left) and Roger Maris (right).

Have two men on the same team hit 50 home runs in the same season?

It has only happened once. The Yankees' famous M & M boys, Mickey Mantle and Roger Maris, did it in 1961. That was the year Roger Maris hit 61 home runs to break Babe Ruth's record of 60. Mickey Mantle hit 54 that same year.

How great this accomplishment is, aside from the fact that it has happened only once, is more obvious when it is noted that only seven other players in the entire history of baseball have hit over 50 home runs in a season. The Babe did it four times. Jimmy Foxx, Willie Mays, Mickey Mantle and Ralph Kiner, twice. Maris, Hank Greenberg, Hack Wilson and Johnny Mize did it once.

When Roger Maris hit that record-breaking No. 61 off Tracy Stallard, a Boston right-hander, the struggle in the stands to get the ball was for more than baseball sentiment. A Sacramento, California restaurant owner had offered $5,000 for the ball Maris hit—such was the excitement surrounding this event. Strangely enough, the fans did not exactly relish (nor did Maris) the breaking of Ruth's record. The fans themselves probably would have chosen Mantle for this favored role. Both Maris and Mantle retired the same year, Maris to a beer distributorship in Florida and Mantle to the restaurant business.

16

Warren Spahn   Denton (Cy) Young   Johnny Vander Meer

How many pitchers have won more than three hundred games?

Warren Spahn recently brought the list to 14. He joined Grover Cleveland Alexander, John Clarkson, James Galvin, Robert Moses Grove, Walter Johnson, Tim Keefe, Christy Mathewson, Charles Nichols, Eddie Plank, Charles Radbourne, Michael Welch, Early Wynn and Denton (Cy) Young. "Spahnie" chalked up 363 wins in 21 seasons to become the winningest left-hander in major-league history. In the process he won 20 or more games in 12 seasons. As great as that was, it was still a far cry from Cy Young's record of 511 wins compiled in 22 sessions.

If you going to make comparisons, though, just remember that Walter Johnson won 416 games in 21 seasons with Washington, a team that earned for that city the label of "First in war, first in peace, and last in the American League."

How many pitchers have hurled no-hitters in both leagues?

Only two—Jim Bunning and Cy Young. Jim Bunning pitched his first for the Detroit Tigers against the Boston Red Sox on July 20, 1958. Then, when he went to the Philadelphia Phils in 1964, he threw his second no-hitter against the New York Mets on June 21, 1964—and made it a perfect game, too.

Cy Young no-hit Cincinnati of the National League, while pitching for Cleveland on Sept. 18, 1897, and then repeated against Philadelphia on May 5, 1904 while pitching for Boston. By a strange coincidence, his second no-hitter was also a perfect game. But it didn't end there for Young. He added a third no-hitter against the Yankees on June 30, 1908.

Young's three no-hitters stood alongside Bob Feller's as a record until the great Sandy Koufax posted four. The first for Koufax came against the New York Mets on June 30, 1962. His second, on May 11, 1963, came against the Giants. The third, on June 4, 1964, was against the Phillies. And the record-breaking fourth was on September 10, 1965, against the Chicago Cubs. It's hard to say that even this feat is the greatest effort in no-hit history. Many experts feel that when Johnny Vander Meer threw consecutive no-hitters, that was the greatest. Vander Meer, while pitching for Cincinnati in 1938, no-hit Boston on June 11, and four days later he throttled the Brooklyn Dodgers!

While on the subject of no-hitters, let's not overlook the fact that, in addition to Vander Meer, Allie Reynolds in a Yankee uniform and Virgil Trucks while pitching for Detroit also delivered two no-hitters in one season. Trucks did it in 1952 against Washington and the Yankees, while Reynolds did it in 1951 against Cleveland and Boston.

We mentioned Bob Feller fleetingly in connection with no-hitters, but he deserves more space than that. Feller is the only pitcher who threw a

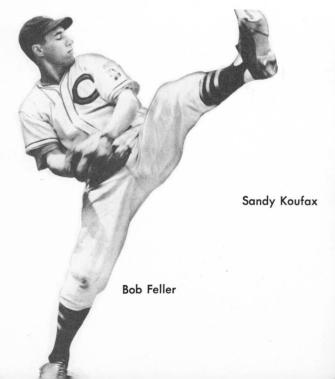

Bob Feller

Sandy Koufax

no-hitter on opening day on the way to making his total of three. And while we're taking note of only's, Alva (Bobo) Holloman is the only rookie making his first major-league start to have turned the no-hitter trick. It didn't help much. Before the end of his first and last season in the big leagues, he had been farmed out.

In closing the subject of no-hitters, two other baseball feats deserve mention. Harvey Haddix of the Pittsburgh Pirates joined the list of all-time hard-luck pitchers on the night of May 26, 1959, when he mowed down the Milwaukee Braves one-two-three for 12 innings. The first hitter for the Braves got on base on an error in the 13th, and after a sacrifice and an intentional walk, Joe Adcock's double turned the no-hitter into a one-hit one-nothing defeat. And how about this one: Jim Vaughn pitched a nine-inning no-hitter, but his mound opponent, Fred Toney, pitched a ten-inning no-hitter with one out in the 10th. Vaughn finally gave up a hit. Let me add a third. The great Babe Ruth one day started a ball game against Washington, but when the first man up got a base on balls, Ruth became so incensed at the umpire that he was thrown out of the game. He was relieved by pitcher Ernie Shore. The runner at first tried to steal second, but didn't make it, and was out. Shore then retired the next 26 men and was given credit for a perfect game!

How is a pitcher's ERA rated?

If a pitcher has an ERA (earned-run average) of 1.00, it means that he has allowed an average of one earned run for every nine innings he has pitched. To determine a pitcher's ERA, divide the total number of innings pitched by nine, and then divide that figure into the total number of earned runs charged to the pitcher.

The all-time major-league leader in lowest earned-run average among pitchers who have won more than two hundred games is Grover Cleveland Alexander. He takes honors with an ERA of 2.56 for 696 games. It's ironic that Alexander is remembered more for the fact that he came in to strike out Tony Lazzeri of the Yankees in the 1926 World Series while pitching for the St. Louis Cards.

While Alexander holds the lifetime ERA record, a little-known pitcher named Ferd Schupp holds the season record with an ERA of 0.90. Schupp's record, though, was based on only 140 innings. Next lowest is Bob Gibson, with 1.12 in 305 innings in 1968. Grover Alexander in 1915 had an ERA of 1.22 in 376 innings. (Incidentally, Hollywood once made a motion picture based on Alexander's life, and the actor who played the part of this all-time great pitcher was Ronald Reagan, who subsequently became governor of California.)

Still in the ERA record category, Lefty Grove led his league nine times, the most by any pitcher, and only one pitcher led both leagues in ERA. Hoyt Wilhelm, pitching for the Giants in 1952, led the National League, and then, while with Baltimore, in the American League in 1959, earned the distinction of leading that league, too.

Who struck out the most men in a lifetime?

Way out in front—as a matter of fact, the only pitcher in the three-thousand strike-out category—is the immortal Walter Johnson. This great, gentle human being used only one pitch, a fast ball . . . but *what* a fast ball! Al Schacht, known as the "clown prince of baseball," was a team-mate of Johnson's. On many occasions Al has said that if Johnson had just a little meanness in him, no one could have hit him.

It was of Johnson that the story was told concerning a player who once went to the bench after only two strikes. The umpire called him back to the plate, reminding him, "You've still got a strike coming." "No, thanks," said the hitter. "That's all I want to see of him."

Years later, another fireballing right-hander, pitching in a pre-season game against the St. Louis Cardinals, brought the same reaction. He was from Van Meter, Iowa, and bore the name of Robert Feller. Rapid Robert set some fancy records in his time. One year he struck out 348 men. On October 2, 1938, he claimed 18 strike-outs in one afternoon.

There are those who insist that the baseball years Feller lost while in the service of his country would have been his greatest. One thing is certain: even without those years, he left quite a mark. It wasn't until a handsome young left-hander from the Flatbush section of Brooklyn appeared on the scene that Feller's name was erased at the top of the strike-out list for a season's play. That lefty—Sandy Koufax—notched 382 strike-outs in 1965 for the all-time record. In the entire history of baseball there have been only three pitchers to strike out more than three hundred men in a season: Bob Feller, Sandy Koufax and a colorful left-hander named Rube Waddell. Waddell struck out 343 men in 1904. Actually, though, even earlier—in 1886—there was a pitcher named Matthew Kilroy who struck out 505 men while pitching for Baltimore. Yes, Kilroy was there, but here's the catch: the distance from the pitcher's mound to the plate was only 50 feet. Today it's 60 feet 6 inches.

What pitcher broke a record in 1968 that had lasted for 55 years?

That pitcher was Don Drysdale of the Los Angeles Dodgers. Don pitched 58 consecutive shut-out innings to break the 56 mark Walter Johnson had set back in 1913. Drysdale actually broke another mark along the way that was of even longer duration—he pitched six consecutive shut-out games. The old record was five, recorded in 1904 by G. Harris White. For Drysdale this record had to be the highlight of his career. Johnson, however, still holds first place in the lifetime shut-out circle—he is the only man to have recorded more than a hundred shut-outs in a lifetime. The total comes to 113.

Don Drysdale

Sequence pictures showing the pitching form of Don Larsen.

What is considered the greatest game ever pitched?

You would get arguments here, but if you feel that the World Series is the time when clutch performers really come to the front, then Don Larsen's masterpiece for the Yankees in the fifth game of the 1956 World Series gets the nod. Sal Maglie started for the Brooklyn Dodgers, and he had a perfect game going, too—until the fourth inning. With one out, Mickey Mantle smacked a homer. That was all Larsen needed, but the Yankees got him another run in the seventh and Maglie wound up pitching a five-hitter, normally a winning effort. Larsen, who had been shelled off the mound in the second inning of the second game, was so superb in his control that only one hitter—Pee Wee Reese, in the first inning—carried the count to three balls. In all, Larsen threw only 97 pitches. In the ninth inning, with two out and 64,519 fans in Yankee Stadium holding their breath, Dale Mitchell was sent in to pinch-hit for Sal Maglie. With the count one ball, two strikes, Mitchell fouled off the next pitch. Then Larsen, using his "no wind-up" delivery, threw another fast ball. Mitchell started to swing, stopped—and Umpire Babe Pinelli, working behind the plate in his last World Series before retiring, called strike three. 27 men up, 27 men down. Larsen had carved out a special niche in World Series history, the only man to pitch a perfect game.

Only seven other men have pitched perfect games since 1900. In that exclusive list we find Cy Young, Boston vs. Philadelphia (AL), in 1904; Adrian Joss, Cleveland vs. Chicago (AL), in 1908; Ernie Shore, Boston vs. Washington (AL), in 1917; C. C. Robertson, Chicago vs. Detroit (AL), in 1922; James Bunning, Philadelphia vs. New York (NL) in 1964; Sandy Koufax, Los Angeles vs. Chicago (NL), in 1965; and Jim (Catfish) Hunter, Oakland vs. Minnesota (AL), in 1968.

Who almost pitched a no-hitter in a World Series?

Floyd Bevens was the Yankee pitcher who came too close to baseball immortality. Although he had been wild, putting himself in trouble often, Bevens had silenced the Brooklyn bats for eight innings. Two of the many bases on balls he issued had paved the way for a Brooklyn run in the fifth. The Yankees, however, had scored twice, so that Bevens was protecting a 2-1 lead as well as striving for the no-hitter as the last of the ninth opened.

Bruce Edwards, the lead-off batter, flied out. Bevens then gave up his ninth walk to Carl Furillo. Spider Jorgensen popped out in foul territory to George McQuinn. Only one out to go! But Al Gionfriddo, a pinch-runner for Furillo, swiped second, running as Brooklyn had throughout the Series on Yogi Berra, who was then inexperienced behind the plate. Pete Reiser, who had an injured leg, was batting for Hugh Casey. With first base now empty, Yankee manager Bucky Harris ordered an intentional pass to Reiser, which meant the winning run was on base.

Eddie Stanky was up next. Even though the second baseman was a sharp-eyed batter, the Dodger mastermind, Burt Shotton, pulled a surprise by sending up another right-handed swinger, veteran Harry ("Cookie") Lavagetto. Cookie banged a double off the right-field wall, scoring the two runners, and not only did Bevens see his no-hit masterpiece demolished, but he also lost the game, 3-2. The pinch two-bagger proved to be Lavagetto's only safety of the Series. The luckless Bevens was left with a dubious entry in the record book—most walks by a pitcher, 10.

Has only one left-hander won three games in a World Series?

The answer is yes. And that lefty is Harry ("The Cat") Brecheen. Pitching for the St. Louis Cardinals against the Boston Red Sox in the 1946 World Series, Brecheen won three games. Even Whitey Ford, the winningest pitcher in World Series history, and Sandy Koufax, as well as Bob Grove, couldn't do it. But there are plenty of right-handers who have done it. Christy Mathewson of the New York Giants and Jack Coombs of the Philadelphia Athletics turned the trick in only a five-game series—Matty in 1905 and Coombs in 1910. Urban Faber won three in a six-game World Series for the Chicago White Sox in 1917. In a seven-game World Series, Babe Adams of Pittsburgh in 1909, Stan Coveleski of Cleveland in 1920, Lew Burdette of Milwaukee in 1957, and Bob Gibson of the 1967 St. Louis Cardinals are the standard-bearers. There are three pitchers who did it when the Series went to eight games. Deacon Phillippe of Pittsburgh and Bill Dinneen of Boston did it in 1903, and Smokey Joe Wood produced three wins for Boston in 1912.

Did Babe Ruth ever pitch in a World Series?

And how! The Babe won three games and never lost one in his World Series appearances as a pitcher. He was involved in the longest game won by a World Series pitcher. In 1916, the Babe outpitched Sherry Smith of Brooklyn and gave Boston a 2-1 victory. More than that, until Whitey Ford came along to break it, Ruth held the record for consecutive scoreless innings in World Series play. The Babe pitched 29 of them. Ford (another lefty) erased the mark by extending the streak to 33⅔ innings before he was scored on by wonderful Willie Mays.

We started this by talking about Babe Ruth. He holds one World Series record that may never be broken. He got ten hits—including three doubles and three homers in sixteen times at bat—in the 1928 Series for a .625 batting average as the Yanks swept the St. Louis Cardinals in four games.

Which pitcher holds the record for most strike-outs in a World Series game?

If you said Bob Gibson, you are right. This superb right-hander, who was a good-enough basketball player to be a member of the Harlem Globetrotters, took the Sandy Koufax record of 15 off the books in the first game of the 1968 World Series. The background for the game was really unusual. Gibson had had an outstanding year, winning 22 and losing 9 with a 1.12 ERA. But even these accomplishments were overshadowed by his mound opponent, Denny McLain. McLain had done something no pitcher had done in 37 years—he had won 31 games. Faced with this challenge, Gibson rose to the occasion like the true champion he is. He bested McLain and the Detroit Tigers, 4-0, and en route struck out 17 men. Bob actually set another strike-out record: his total of 35 strike-outs is the most ever in one series.

The record for most strike-outs by one pitcher for total World Series is held by Whitey Ford of the Yankees at 94. You might have noticed by now that Whitey Ford's name appears quite a few times when one gets into World Series pitching records. Just checking it out, you realize that if there's such a thing as a World Series pitcher, it's gotta be Whitey. Here are

Whitey Ford

Bob Gibson

his records: most World Series (11), most World Series games (22), most wins (10), most losses (8), most innings pitched (146), most bases on balls (34), along with the aforementioned most strikeouts in total World Series and most consecutive scoreless innings. What makes Whitey's records seem tough to break is that it doesn't seem likely that another team could so dominate a league as the Yankees once did, and so another pitcher may never get the chances Whitey had. And it's not only a matter of pitchers, but in other categories, too. For example, there's Yogi Berra, who has been in 14 World Series as a player. Yogi was on ten winners, went to bat 259 times, got 71 hits, 49 of them singles (a record). But all of this took place when the big question was, "Who's going to play the Yankees in the World Series?" Since no team is likely to repeat the Yankee successes, no ball player would get the chance.

Catcher Yogi Berra

What was Bobby Thomson's "shot heard round the world"?

Even if you weren't around in 1951, you may have heard of baseball's "shot heard round the world." It happened this way. The New York Giants, managed by Leo Durocher, had staged a "miracle" comeback to tie the Brooklyn Dodgers for the pennant. Now there had to be a play-off— best two of three games. The Giants won the first, 3-1. Back came the Dodgers to win the second, 10-0. It was all on the line that fateful day at the Polo Grounds. Going to the bottom of the ninth inning, it was 4-1 in favor of the Dodgers. Forgotten was the fact that the Brooklyns had blown a thirteen-and-a-half game lead they had in August. All big Don Newcombe,

Bobby Thomson hitting the homer that won the final play-off game (and the National League pennant) in 1951 against the Brooklyn Dodgers.

the Dodgers ace right-hander, had to do was get three men. You could hear the Dodger fans in the Polo Grounds screaming, "Get 'em, Newk!"

First up for the Giants in the bottom half of the ninth was Alvin Dark. He got an infield hit. When Don ("Mandrake") Mueller singled, putting runners on first and third, the Giant fans began to roar. Monte Irvin popped up...and things quieted down. But not for long. Whitey Lockman doubled, driving in Dark and making the score 4-2. On the play Mueller sprained his ankle sliding into third and had to be carried off the field. Clint Hartung (The Hondo Hurricane) went in as a pinch-runner. Dodger manager Chuck Dressen then made the decision to bring in Ralph Branca, in relief of Newcombe. Up to bat came Bobby Thomson, the Staten Island Scot, as he was called. The issue wasn't in doubt long. Branca got his first pitch over for a strike. His second pitch resulted in "the shot heard round the world." Thomson hit the shot into the left-field stands for a three-run homer that won the game, 5-4.

As you might expect, there were some who thought Dodger manager Dressen should have walked Thomson to get at the next hitter. But Chuck had simply followed the book: never put the winning run on base. Incidentally, the batter on deck for the Giants that day was their rookie center-fielder, a fellow named Willie Mays.

Willie Mays sends a shot to the stands.

Carl Hubbell, master of the screwball.

Who inaugurated the All-Star Game?

The All-Star Game was the brainchild of Arch Ward, sports editor of the *Chicago Tribune,* who conceived of such a game in 1933. It has since become one of the major annual attractions of baseball. There was no game in 1945 because of governmental (wartime) restrictions on traveling. Two All-Star Games were played in 1959, and this practice continued through 1962; then the majors returned to a single game in 1963. At first, the stars to represent the American and National League were selected by a vote of the fans, but this system was abandoned in favor of having the players chosen by league executives and managers. Voting by fans was resumed in 1947, but again abandoned, and players, coaches and managers became the selectors. Two men who have seen most service in All-Star Games were Stan Musial for the National League, who participated in 24 games, and Ted Williams for the American League, who appeared in 18 games. These two players combined eminence with longevity. As a matter of fact, Ted Williams, Early Wynn and Mickey Vernon share the distinction of having played in the 1930's, 40's, 50's and 60's. The highest batting average produced by players with at least 20 at-bats in All-Star Games is a .500 mark for Charlie Gehringer of the American League and a .433 average for Billie Herman of the National League. Both were second basemen. You're probably wondering, "What about Willie Mays?" Some say that wonderful Willie is the greatest all-star participant of them all. Through 1968, Willie had the most hits, 23, and the most stolen bases, 6. He also had scored the most runs, 19. It is doubtful that anyone, including Arch Ward, foresaw the quality of baseball that was to flow at these games, particularly in those early days when the American League dominated the Nationals. With a Lefty Gomez perennially winning under an umbrella of support provided by the likes of Babe Ruth (who hit a home run in the first game) and other assorted American League sluggers, it looked as if the National League would never catch up—but it did. There have been so many heroes, one is almost unwilling to name them, for fear of leaving someone out. But let's march on fearlessly. Gomez and Ruth and Hubbell. And how, Hubbell!

It was the second game played in all-star competition. (The date— July 10, 1934.) On the mound for the National League was the Oklahoma southpaw. The arm which looked pretzel-twisted from throwing so many screwballs belonged to Carl Hubbell. There was no hint of the superlative feat that was to come from the way in which Hubbell started. Charlie Gehringer opened the game with a sharp single. Hubbell then walked Heinie Manush. Two men on, nobody out, and Babe Ruth at the plate. The crooked arm flailed the air and Ruth struck out on three pitches. "Iron Man" Lou Gehrig was next. He went down swinging. The Maryland strongboy, Jimmy Foxx, then dug in at the plate and became the third strike-out victim. More to come. Al Simmons, "foot-in-the-bucket" Simmons, led off for the American League in the second and whiffed. Joe Cronin became victim No. 5. Bill Dickey then broke the spell and lined a single. Lefty Gomez, the gay caballero—admittedly not much of a hitter, even for a pitcher—quickly became strike-out No. 6 as Hubbell wrapped up the finest two innings of mound work in All-Star history.

Then there was a July 8 game in 1941, with the American League down by two runs in the bottom of the ninth inning. A young splinter —they called him the "splendid splinter"—came to the plate and hit a towering home run to win the game for the American League. His name was Ted Williams, and the mark of greatness was on him, even at that young age. He was all of 22, and would go on that year to become a .400 hitter —.406, to be exact.

Then there was the seventeenth game of the series played by the all-stars, the one at Chicago that went 14 innings. It occurred on July 11, 1950, and the man who now manages the St. Louis Cardinals, Red Schoendienst, hit one into the seats to win it. That was the one in which Ralph Kiner (now a sports announcer) tied it up in the ninth for the National League. Earlier, in the first inning, Kiner had smashed a ball to left field that Ted Williams pulled down running into the wall. X-ray photographs taken the following day disclosed that Williams had suffered a fracture of the left elbow. Despite the pain, he had continued to play until the ninth inning, when he singled in a run to give the American League a short-lived 3-to-2 lead. That's quality that makes the difference.

Don't get the idea that all the good games were played long ago. In 1967—on another July 11, coincidentally, but this time in Anaheim, California—they played for 15 innings before the National League won it 2 to 1. Don Drysdale and Jim ("Catfish") Hunter were the pitchers of record, Drysdale getting the win and Hunter the loss. A year later Drysdale was to set the all-time record for consecutive shut-out innings at 58 and Hunter was to become one of the select few who have pitched a perfect game.

And so it goes. The list is so long that to have named just a handful may seem unjust. I feel somewhat like a man who has been granted three wishes by a genie, and now that I've taken them, I just wish I had more. But for those whose deeds have gone unrecorded here, there is the consolation that their fans will always remember them. They were all great. They were *all* All-Stars.

Action during the Lehigh-Lafayette game in 1889.

Football

Who invented football?

For younger readers, something should be made clear. Football was not invented by Joe Namath on January 12, 1969 at the Orange Bowl in Miami. True, "Broadway Joe" left an indelible mark on the game that day as he led his teammates to the first American League victory in the Super Bowl. In the afterglow of the upset win, Namath was credited with everything. But no, he did not invent football. As a matter of fact, deciding who invented football is something like deciding who invented baseball, except that football never was involved with a Doubleday myth.

31

Like baseball, football springs from English roots—soccer, or association football, and Rugby. Soccer actually did not originate in England. In one form or another, that game has been played for several thousand years. Rugby, the historians tell us, is an English game. It originated accidentally in 1823 when William Ellis, a student at Rugby College, was involved in an interclass football (soccer) game. In those days one could only kick the ball. Ellis, a bit unhappy with his play, picked up the ball and ran with it. He received a great deal of criticism for this rash act, but when word spread regarding whathe had done, some players felt that running as well as kicking would make the game a better one . . . and so, Rugby came into being. There are some historians, notably Professor H. A. Giles, who assert that a game of football was played by the Chinese sometime from 300 B.C. to A.D. 500. In ancient Greece, a football game called *Harpaston* was popular.

The game as we know it today had its beginnings in 1869. That was the year Rutgers and Princeton pioneered intercollegiate football at New Brunswick, New Jersey, playing games on successive Saturdays, November 6 and November 13. Rutgers won the first, 6 to 4, and Princeton won the second, 8 to 0. After that came the deluge of football. And with that deluge came an outpouring of language that has confounded most people. Let's try unraveling it.

What is the single-wing?

The single-wing gets its name from the positioning of its backfield. It usually has an unbalanced line, meaning there are more players on one side of the center than the other. In this formation the blocking back (the single-wing quarterback) is about a yard and a half behind the line and between the right guard and right tackle. The wingback, from whom single-wing comes, is like a flanker in the "T" formation except that he is closer to the end, about two yards outside and one yard behind. The fullback is about four yards directly behind the center, and the tailback is about four and a half yards behind.

Scene from Columbia's startling 7-0 upset over Stanford in the Rose Bowl on New Year's Day, 1934.

What is the basic "T" formation?

Again, the formation gets its name from the way the backfield lines up in relation to the line. In the basic "T," the line formation has three men on either side of the center (a balanced line). The center, who is in the middle of the line, forms the bottom of the "T." The quarterback is immediately behind him. The fullback is about three and a half yards behind the center and is flanked by two halfbacks who are about three yards behind their respective tackles.

What is the winged "T"?

This formation is sort of a compromise between the single-wing and the basic "T" formation. If you can picture the single-wing with the quarterback under center and the fullback and tailback side by side, you've got it. Or, if you can, picture instead the "T" formation with one of the halfbacks moved out as a wingback. Same difference.

What is the pro "T"?

Professional football has grown by leaps and bounds because it has satisfied the one demand the fans have placed on it: throw the football. The pro "T" formation gives the quarterback a chance to get his receivers in position to receive quickly. When we talked about the winged "T," we mentioned that one of the halfbacks went out on the wing. In the pro "T," this man widens the gap between himself and the end, so now we have a flanker. On the other side of the formation the end is also split wide. So now we have the split end. And that's basically the pro "T." Of course, the setbacks (those who remain behind the quarterback) can also be moved around. That's where slotting a back comes in. You take one of those setbacks and put him in the slot between the flanker and end or between the split end and the line. All you're doing is getting more men in position to go downfield and become receivers.

What is an odd defense? What is an even defense?

It's really quite simple. Whenever a defensive man is over the head of the offensive center, he is in an odd defense. If not, he is in an even. Most professional defenses are even defenses with the defensive tackles lined up over the offensive guards and the defensive ends lined up over the offensive tackles. The middle linebacker is just that—he is behind the defensive line and in its middle. The outside linebackers play outside the ends and behind them. The cornerbacks are at the corners of the defense, guarding against the flanker and split end. The strong safety lines up to guard against the tight end. The weak safety is so-called because there is no end on his side close to the line. That end is being watched by a cornerback so that sometimes the weak safety is called the free safety.

What is a zone defense? What is a man for man?

First, man for man. As you might have guessed from the name, each man in the defensive backfield has a particular offensive man to guard, no matter where he goes. In the zone defense, the players are assigned a particular zone. Those zones are designated by the "hash marks" on the field, the lines dividing the field in three parts. Hash marks are sometimes called the in-bounds markers. They are one-third of the way in from the sidelines. That divides the field into three equal zones.

Tommy Harmon (98) making one of his long runs for Michigan U.

What is a blitz?

You've probably heard it referred to as a "red dog," or "plugging the gap," but no matter how or what it's called, all it means is that one of your linebackers, or sometimes your safety man, crashes through the offensive blocking to get at the quarterback. When you hear different colors used to designate a particular blitz, all it means is that a different player is being designated as the blitzer.

What is an eligible receiver?

All the men in the backfield and the men stationed at both ends of the line are eligible. You may have heard the term in "tackle eligible." This is a cute way for getting your offensive tackle eligible to receive, and is done by dropping the end on his side back off the line so that he is now in the backfield. The wingback comes up on the line of scrimmage and now you have the "tackle eligible."

When was the forward pass first introduced to football?

Historians have excavated an account of how the first forward pass came into being in a story of the Yale-Princeton game of November 30, 1876. The brief mention indicated that the ball was thrown forward after a player with possession had been tackled.

Another account of a game between the same rivals in 1883 indicated that the ball was thrown 25 feet after it was snapped from center. Thus, perhaps, grew the concept of the modern forward pass.

The next incident of a forward pass took place in a Georgia-North Carolina game in 1895. The Carolina fullback got the ball and was undecided what to do with it. The Georgia players expected a kick and rushed the fullback, who had instructions to get rid of the ball fast, as far down field as possible. He took a few steps to one side and threw a short distance forward to one of the players, who went 70 yards for a touchdown.

Whenever the first forward pass was thrown, it was obviously a long time ago, and how it happened is an academic question. The passing attack as we know it today was perfected by two men, Charlie ("Gus") Dorais, the passer, and Knute Rockne, the No. 1 receiver, on the 1912-13 Notre Dame teams.

In 1913, against Army at West Point, they introduced the passing attack to the East. Dorais threw 21 passes and completed 17 of them for

243 yards. The wide-open style of attack, which gained big yardage, baffled the cadets who had expected an old-fashioned, line-smashing game. The Irish won, 35 to 13, with all five touchdowns being set up or scored on passes.

Is O. J. Simpson the greatest runner of them all?

Answering this question is like deciding whether athletes today are as good or better than the old-timers. If you think the old-timers were better, then you'll start throwing names like Willie Heston, Jim Thorpe, Ernie Nevers, Red Grange, Tom Harmon, Glenn Davis and Doc Blanchard at those who are for O. J. About the soundest argument I've heard is the one that says that great athletes are great in their time, and to compare athletes of different eras just doesn't make sense. It's tough enough making comparisons of athletes of the same era. For example, do you think that O. J. is a better runner than Gale Sayers or Jimmy Brown? If you're one of those "figure filberts," and that's the basis for

Knute Rockne showing a Notre Dame player how to block an opponent.

Gale Sayers

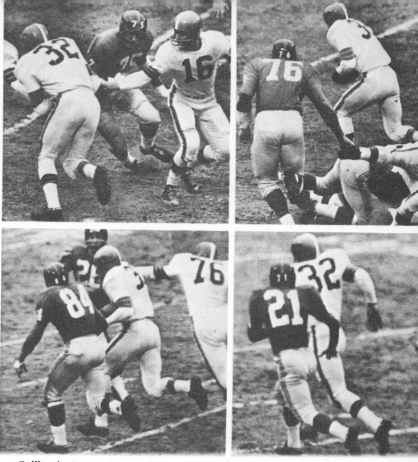

Fullback Jimmy Brown (32) gets the handoff and heads for a 65-yard touchdown run.

your arguments, then you've got a strong case for O. J. The great Southern California back ran for more yardage in just two years of major college ball (he had one year of junior college) than all but five men in football history. In 1968, he ran for 1,709 yards, a single-season record for yards gained rushing. That, plus his 1,415 yards gained the previous year, gave him a grand total of 3,124 yards gained in just two years, by far the most yardage ever gained in two years. That total placed him sixth on the all-time rushing list, a list that included some who had gained their yardage in four years of play.

O. J.'s size (six feet two, 210 pounds) plus his blazing speed (9.3 in track competition) made him ideally suited for his job. Add to that his great balance and broken-field agility, and the picture is complete. If there was ever a man perfectly made for running, it's O. J. Simpson. But is he the greatest? I think the answer is that he's the greatest college runner of them all. Now he's got to add the professional statistics and the answer should be complete.

Roy Riegels, seated on the ground, is disconsolate after his "wrong-way" run at the Rose Bowl on January 1, 1929.

Who was "Wrong Way" Riegels?

Roy Riegels was the center and captain of the University of California Golden Bears, and he was involved in one of those episodes that have become football legend. It all happened in the Rose Bowl game of 1929, and seventy thousand fans in the stands witnessed it. In the second quarter, Riegels picked up a Georgia Tech fumble and started toward the Tech goal line. A platoon of Tech players sprung up around Riegels, and in trying to get away from them he cut back across the field. He apparently became confused and started toward his own goal line, 60 yards away. Players from both teams stood amazed as he ran down the sidelines. Benny Lom, a halfback for California, took off after Riegels, who turned on more speed as he heard footsteps behind him. Finally, the speedier Lom caught him, but not before he had gotten to the three-yard line—*his own* three-yard line! He was tackled there by a swarm of Georgia Tech players. California went into punt formation. The kick was blocked and Georgia Tech got a safety, which proved to be the difference, as they won the ball game, 8-7.

The famed Four Horsemen of Notre Dame: (left to right) Harry Stuhldreher, Don Miller, Jim Crowley and Elmer Layden.

How did the "Four Horsemen" term originate?

Grantland Rice, one of the greatest sports writers ever, coined the phrase in 1924 when Notre Dame defeated Army, 13-7, before 55,000 spectators at the Polo Grounds in New York. What Rice wrote in his lead has become sports-writing literature—words many present-day sports writers wish they had written. This was Rice's lead paragraph:

"Outlined against a blue-gray October sky, the Four Horsemen rode again. In dramatic lore they are known as Famine, Pestilence, Destruction and Death. These are only aliases. Their real names are Stuhldreher, Miller, Crowley and Layden. They formed the crest of the South Bend cyclone before which another fighting Army football team was swept over the precipice at the Polo Grounds yesterday afternoon . . ."

Rice later wrote that the idea for the phrase had been planted in his mind a year earlier when Army played Notre Dame at Ebbets Field in Brooklyn. Rice watched the game from the sidelines because he only had a sidelines pass. On one wild end run the whole Notre Dame backfield swarmed over the sidelines where Rice was standing. The Irish backs swept right through Rice, who had fallen to his knees. "It's worse than a cavalry charge," he said to a friend. "They're like a wild-horse stampede!" The thought occurred to him again the next year in the press box at the Polo Grounds and he ticked it off on his typewriter. That's how the phrase "Four Horsemen" was born.

Felix ("Doc") Blanchard, running in the clear.

Glenn Davis (left) and Felix Blanchard (right), "Mr. Outside" and "Mr. Inside," respectively.

Who were Mr. Inside and Mr. Outside?

Felix ("Doc") Blanchard and Glenn Davis. Blanchard played fullback and Davis halfback for the Army teams from 1944 to 1946. These two young men ran roughshod over opponents for three years. In 1944, the Cadets went undefeated in nine games, scoring an astounding total of 504 points against only 35. Entering their last college game against Navy in 1946, Blanchard, whose power enabled him to carry would-be tacklers along with him, and Davis, a swift, elusive runner, had engineered the Army teams to a three-year record of 26 wins and a tie against Notre Dame. They were also known as the Touchdown Twins.

Who once made four long touchdown runs in the first ten minutes?

Harold ("Red") Grange, the "Galloping Ghost" of Illinois, turned in one of the most memorable performances ever seen on a football field against Michigan at Urbana, Illinois, on October 18, 1924.

The flashing red-haired "pheenom" had been named an All-American the year before. He thrilled a crowd of 67,000 in single-handedly routing the Wolverines, 39-14.

(Left) Harold ("Red") Grange, the immortal "77" at the University of Illinois. (Above) Bronko Nagurski, all-time football great.

On the opening kick-off, Grange tore through the Michigan team for 95 yards and a touchdown. The game was little more than ten seconds old. Before the Wolverines could recover from the shock, Grange had galloped for 66, 55, and 40 yards. He even had time to leave to a thunderous ovation before the first quarter was over. He returned in the third quarter and scored a fifth touchdown on a fifteen-yard run, and in the fourth quarter he passed 23 yards for the last Illinois score. In all, he handled the ball 21 times and gained 402 yards. Grange was a baffling-type runner who could untangle himself from clusters of would-be tacklers when it seemed that he was hopelessly trapped.

As great as he was, he was virtually unknown in the East. Unknown, that is, until he hit Philadelphia on October 31, 1925 to play against the University of Pennsylvania. Grange proved that he was no myth. He slipped and twisted and turned from tacklers for three touchdowns as the Illini humbled Penn 24-2. Twice he went 60 yards for scores, and on his third touchdown he went 24 tough yards. In all, he gained 363 yards. The "Galloping Ghost" had done it again.

Who did they call "Bronko"?

There may have been others who were called Bronko, but when you say that name and you mean football, there was only one, Bronko Nagurski. They tell the story that when "Doc" Spears, the Minnesota coach, found him, Nagurski was a raw-boned farm boy. Spears was trying to get directions to Duluth. "Which way to Duluth?" Spears is supposed to have yelled. The boy on the farm pointed—with his plow. Before he was through, Nagurski had pointed the way for the University of Minnesota and for the Chicago Bears. "The Bronk" was really unbelievable. It's sometimes hard to separate fact from fiction about him. One year he sustained an injury to his back, and since he couldn't bend over to play fullback, they put him on the line as tackle. He was just as good. When he bucked the line, it stayed bucked. For many years the record for most yards gained in the National Football League was held by a halfback named Beattie Feathers. He played for the Chicago Bears, running behind the blocking of Bronko Nagurski. Coach Jeff Cravath of Rice once said, "Eleven Nagurskis would wreck any other one-man team." It should be mentioned about the Bronk that he started as an end, switched to tackle and made All-American—and then switched to fullback and made All-American. They said of him that he ran his own interference. He was a rare one.

What football player became a Justice of the U.S. Supreme Court?

A really great one named Whizzer White. He could do it all on a football field. He played for the University of Colorado where he had gone on an academic rather than a football scholarship. In 1937, Whizzer put Colorado on the football map. He led the country in scoring, rushing, and total offense. He was a fast shifty runner, strong enough to run over you if he had to. And in those days, when you had to play both ways, he did. He was a tremendous punter and he kicked extra points and field goals. They

Byron ("Whizzer") White, pictured in 1937 as a star football player at the University of Colorado. He became a Rhodes scholar and a pro football star in later days—and eventually became an associate justice on the U. S. Supreme Court.

tell the story about how Whizzer, who once had just made a fine run, thought that the official had called a play wrong. He said something about it to the official and it cost his team fifteen yards. There was another penalty called against the Colorado team and it backed them up almost to their goal line. But Whizzer took the ball on several running plays and led his team to a score.

As had been the case with Red Grange years before, White's exploits were viewed with doubt in the East. The experts figured that here was a good local boy. Well, Whizzer had his chance to prove his merit when Colorado played in the Cotton Bowl against a fine Rice team that was the champion of the Southwest Conference. Although the Colorado team wasn't the equal of the Rice eleven, White ran for one TD and passed for another. There was no doubt now about how good he was.

And so it was that the Pittsburgh Steelers offered him a chance in the N.F.L. White, though, had been named a Rhodes scholar and it didn't look like he could play pro ball (shades of Bill Bradley). But the Steelers finally convinced him and he played. He led the National League in rushing with a total of 567 yards. Later he played for the Detroit Lions and made All-League. When John F. Kennedy became President of the United States, he named Whizzer White to the Supreme Court.

Who was the greatest all-around player?

This is the easiest way to start a real argument, but if there was a better all-around player than Jim Thorpe, he's been in hiding. What couldn't Thorpe do? Well, let's first talk about what he *could* do. He kicked the ball 80 yards with some frequency. Some old-timers insist they saw him kick it a hundred yards. He could drop kick the football as pretty as you please. And if you wanted, he could kick off. On defense he'd hit you and you might think that you'd been hit by a truck. The same held true for his blocking. Passing was one of those little-used things when he played. But if you played with a football, he could do anything with the ball. Yes, he could pass. Not like Joe Namath, but he could pass. He could catch. And he could run! Remember, this was the man who won the decathlon in the Olympics. Sure, they took his medals away from him because he played some semi-pro baseball, but they couldn't take away what the King of Sweden had said when he gave him those medals in 1912. "You, sir," the monarch said, "are the greatest athlete in the world." And when that greatest athlete in the world took the pigskin in his hand and decided to run with it, he was something to behold. The story is told that when he played against someone who hit extra hard, he'd say, "Don't do that to Old Jim." If the op-

posing player didn't take heed, the big Indian would run over him so hard that the man would have to be carried off the field. That's how hard he ran. And if he wanted to, he'd give you all the fancy stuff, too. The swivel hip, the cut back, the stop and go, the change of pace. They were part of his equipment. He was, as the King of Sweden said, "the greatest athlete in the world."

Jim Thorpe, considered to be the greatest football player who ever lived.

45

But how about the ones who play today?

O.K., you want to know about Bart Starr and Joe Namath and Johnny Unitas and the Green Bay Packers. Let's discuss the Green Bay Packers first.

When you mention the Packers, you've got to mention one man before you ever talk about any of their ball players—Vince Lombardi. Some know him only as a coach, but he was a very fine college football player at Fordham University when that school was one of the powerhouses in the East. That was in 1937, and Vince Lombardi played with the "Seven Blocks of Granite." These linemen were coached by a young man named Frank Leahy, and they were good enough to hold mighty Pittsburgh scoreless. So Lombardi was a member of a good, if not great, team as a player in college. Later he was an assistant coach at West Point under Earl ("Red") Blaik, one of the finest coaches ever.

When he got to Green Bay, he already had experience coaching in the pros with the New York Giants. He put all of that savvy to work at Green Bay, where he took a loser and made it into one of the all-time winners. One of the big reasons was a former University of Alabama quarterback named Bart Starr. Lombardi gave this young man the kind of training that made him great.

Now, there have been many outstanding quarterbacks in pro football —Sammy Baugh, Sid Luckman, Norm Van Brocklin, Otto Graham, Bob Waterfield, to name a few. Starr may not even be as great technically as some of them, but he had that one great quality, being a winner. Will anyone ever forget the way he came up with the big plays against the Dallas Cowboys? Or the way he could pick another team apart with his effective play-calling?

In every respect he was a real champion, both on and off the field.

The man that they call the greatest pro quarterback, though, is a player who was no great shakes in college and was actually on the verge of quitting when he was cut by the Pittsburgh Steelers. That man is Johnny Unitas. When he was cut by the Steelers, he went to work as the "monkey"

(Above) Vince Lombardi as the left guard —and one of the famous "Seven Blocks of Granite"—at Fordham University. (Right) Johnny Unitas, quarterback for the Baltimore Colts.

on a pile-driver and played for the Bloomfield Rams on the side. Then he got his call from the Baltimore Colts and he was ready. Weeb Ewbank, the same man who coached Joe Namath, was at Baltimore when Johnny "U" showed. Two years later the Colts were the champions of the pro football world. The 1958 meeting of the Baltimore Colts and the New York Giants has been called the greatest football game of all time.

It was a dark, chilly day in New York, the way it nearly always is in New York that time of the year. These two great teams had gone at one another like two cinematic prehistoric monsters. Now it was in the fourth period. The lights were on and it really looked weird. Gino Marchetti, one of the best defensive ends the game has ever known, had just fractured his ankle stopping Frank Gifford inches short of a first down, and so the Giants had to kick. Now it was Baltimore's ball with less than two minutes to go, and the Giants leading 17-14. The Colts had to go 86 yards for a touchdown.

The first two passes by Unitas were incomplete, so Unitas did the unexpected. He ran Lenny Moore for 11 yards and a first down. Three more passes missed and the Colts looked dead. But on fourth down, Johnny "U" threw and the great Raymond Berry caught. It was now first down on the

50-yard line. The Colts called time out with 64 seconds remaining. Twice more now Unitas threw to Berry, and with the clock running and no more time-outs left, the ball was on the Giants' 13. Steve Myrha kicked a field goal and it was overtime.

The Giants won the toss and elected to receive, but they could not move the ball. When they kicked, it was Baltimore's ball on the Colts' 20. Make way for Johnny. He moved his team in fitful spurts. Twice on big third-down plays he threw swing passes to his fullback, Alan Ameche, and the big guy just squeezed past the first-down mark. Unitas then showed remarkable calm in the face of a Giant pass rush and hit Raymond Berry on the Giants' 44. Here Unitas displayed field generalship by faking a pass and giving the ball to Alan Ameche. The battering ram took it 24 yards further. The Colts now were in field-goal range. But Unitas was not going for three. He again went to Berry on a slant-in. It took the Colts to the Giant eight. Ameche lowered his head and moved for two. The resistance was fierce. Here again, with no one daring to believe that Unitas could put the ball in the air, that's just what he did. Jim Mutscheller, his tight end, caught it on the one and fell out of bounds before he could get over the goal line.

Joe Namath, dodging the Oakland Raiders' Ben Davidson (83), gets a pass away during the 1968 A.F.L. championship game.

Then Ameche barged over and it was 23-17 Baltimore. There have been other great moments for Unitas, but this one is the prize example of what makes him tick.

And what makes Joe Namath tick? More than any athlete, he is the symbol of his time—rebellious, open, unafraid to speak his mind, Namath reminds the young people of themselves. He's one of them. If he disagrees with the coach, he doesn't hesitate to say so. If he wants to wear his hair long, he wears it long, and if he wants to wear a mustache, he wears a mustache. But if that's all you see in "Broadway Joe," you're missing a lot about him. Always remember that for all of his talk and for all of what seems to be his bragging, he can back it up with what he does on the field. He's not just an idle braggart. He's fortunate in having a great arm. He can throw the ball as well or better than anyone ever. He can throw it long or short, hard or soft, and he's a genius for timing the bomb. All of this didn't come about by sitting and talking about it. From the very time he realized what he could do with a football back in Beaver Falls, Pennsylvania, Joe worked at perfecting his skills. At the University of Alabama the craft was honed even more. But something else happened at Alabama—he got hurt, hurt bad. It was the injuries to his legs that gave Joe even more reckless abandon than he ever had. He didn't know when those injuries would finish him off, and so, instead of making him a conservative player, it added to his flair.

Before the Super Bowl game with the Baltimore Colts, Namath was widely quoted in the papers about how he felt the Jets would beat the Colts. The rest of his teammates felt the same way, only they didn't say it. Joe said it out in the open. It didn't win him any friends, but that never bothered Joe. "I want people to take me for what I am," he said. And what Joe is is a great quarterback. Sometimes the extent of his personality distracts people from that realization. He does all the things that the master Unitas does. He reads defenses as if he had written them. He can throw the ball as well as anyone, and he has no fear (like Unitas throwing when you'd swear he wouldn't dare). But if you're going to be completely objective about it, when you rate an athlete, you've always got to include one factor, and that's longevity. The really great ones, like Starr and Unitas and Otto Graham, did it more than one time. "Joe Willie" will have to repeat, too.

There really should be more mention of Otto Graham. About the best way to explain how wonderful he was is to repeat a story told by George Ratterman. Ratterman had been one of the better quarterbacks in the All-America conference while playing for the Buffalo Bills. When the All-America conference was absorbed by the National Football League, Ratterman finally wound up with the Cleveland Browns—as a benchwarmer. He was asked how it could be that as talented a quarterback as he rarely got into a game. The cherubic-faced athlete never hesitated. "Because Otto Graham is so much better than I am," he said. It kind of took you back to hear someone talk so casually about a situation he was personally involved in. Look at the record. Everywhere that Graham's been and everything he's ever been in, he's been a winner at. Paul Brown might have put it even better. Said Mr. Brown, "The test of a quarterback is where his team finishes." So Otto Graham, by that standard, was the best of all time. But don't get the impression that Graham was just another cog. If you do, it's only because the personality of the man who coached the team, Paul

Brown, was much like that of Vince Lombardi, so dominant that he overshadowed even his players. When you played for Brown, he was the boss and that was that. Graham's greatness was probably underplayed, as Bart Starr's was under Lombardi, because Paul Brown ran his team in similar fashion—perhaps not with the same emotionalism, but with the same singleness of purpose.

Otto Graham, peerless leader of the title-winning Cleveland Browns during the early Fifties.

Where and when was the first pro football game played?

The town of Latrobe, Pennsylvania, about forty miles from Pittsburgh, earns the honor as the site of the first acknowledged pro game. Sponsored by the local Y.M.C.A., the game matched Latrobe against a team from the nearby town of Jeannette. It was played on August 31, 1895. The home team won, 12-0, and the players were paid ten dollars each.

For the next twenty-five years the sport was concentrated mainly in Pennsylvania, Ohio, Indiana, Illinois and New York. Teams were casually organized, scheduling was an impromptu affair, and the better players shifted to wherever the money beckoned. The pay was low, with few getting more than a hundred dollars per game. Many collegians played under pseudonyms on Sundays, after their Saturday varsity efforts. Knute Rockne, after he was graduated from Notre Dame, was supposed to have set some sort of record by playing for six different teams in one season. "Pudge" Heffelfinger of Yale starred later on with a Pittsburgh team, after Pop Warner was a guard on a Syracuse eleven that played in Madison Square Garden on December 28, 1902, and won, 6-0.

That same year, Connie Mack organized his baseball athletics into a football team and claimed the world championship after his club defeated Pittsburgh, 12-6. Pittsburgh had a fullback named Christy Mathewson who had been a football standout at Bucknell and had just started his magnificent baseball career. Heated rivalries sprang up among such Ohio towns as Canton, Akron, Massillon, Columbus and Dayton. The great Jim Thorpe began his pro career with Canton in 1915 and was a terror for the next decade. He had an interesting custom of covering his shoulder pads with sheet metal, which made tackling him a memorable experience. By 1920, the time was thought to be at hand to try to organize the first pro football league. Named the American Professional Football Association, it was the forerunner of the National Football League. Eleven teams joined and the fee was a flat $100. The teams were the Akron Professionals, the

Dayton Triangles, the Cleveland Indians, the Canton Bulldogs, the Massillon Tigers, Rochester (N.Y.), Rock Island (Illinois), Muncie (Indiana), the Chicago Cardinals, and the Decatur (Illinois) Staleys. The meeting took place in the office of Ralph Hays, an auto dealer in Canton, on September 17, 1920. For the value of his name, Thorpe was elected president. However, by April of the next year, the league had to be reorganized, and Joe Carr, a former sports writer and manager of a Columbus team, took over as president, a position he held with distinction until he died in 1939.

Which two teams played the longest pro championship game?

The Dallas Texans and the Houston Oilers in the 1962 A.F.L. title game. After the Texans ran up a 17-0 lead in the first two quarters, the Oilers, with veteran George Blanda at the helm, came back in the second half and evened the score, Blanda converting after Charlie Tolar's one-yard buck early in the final period.

When the quarter ended in a 17-17 deadlock, halfback Abner Haynes, the Dallas Offensive captain, went to mid-field for the coin toss. Haynes was instructed by Coach Hank Stram to pick the end of the field with the wind advantage. Haynes won the toss, but surprisingly said, "We'll kick." So Dallas lost both the advantage of receiving and the wind.

The unintended edge did not help the Oilers to score and the Texans were similarly frustrated through the first 15-minute overtime period, but they had the ball as the period ended.

At the beginning of the second extra period, Len Dawson completed a 10-yard pass to halfback Jack Spikes and Spikes raced for 19 yards to the Houston 19. Rookie Tommy Brooker became the Dallas hero of the day by kicking a 25-yard field goal at 2:58 and the Texans won, 20-17.

James A. Naismith (1861-1939)

Basketball

There are no doubts as to who invented basketball and where. During the summer of 1890, the need for some new game became imperative at Springfield College (known then as the International Y.M.C.A. Training School) in Springfield, Massachusetts. Young coaches and athletic directors had gathered there from many different states for the summer term and all expressed complaints about the lack of interest in their winter gymnasium classes. There was little interest in the type of activity introduced by R. J. Roberts, a one-time circus performer who had inaugurated a system of exercises that he termed body-building work.

The directors of the school agreed that what was needed was an indoor team sport that could compete successfully with football and baseball, which were largely responsible for the Y.M.C.A.'s high summer and fall recruitment of members.

They turned the whole problem over to Dr. James A. Naismith, a Canadian instructor at the school, and they couldn't have picked a better man. Dr. Naismith was the type who went about things methodically. He first examined all outdoor-team sports, and noticed that what most of them had in common was that they used a ball which was driven, thrown, or struck toward a goal. All right, he'd start with a ball, but since the game he was seeking would have to be played indoors, it could not be small and hard like a baseball. An uncontrolled baseball would be dangerous.

Second, he took note that the most popular team sports featured body contact and hard running, both of which would be hazardous in a small area with hard floors. His game would have to be slowed down somehow, with no hard rampant running and embodying a minimum of body contact. Along with this he noticed that the roughest play occurred when one team was near another's goal.

His solutions to these problems? First, use a large, lightweight ball, like a soccer ball, which could be easily controlled and wouldn't damage the players or the premises if it did get out of control. Second, make it illegal to run with the ball (have the man in possession bounce it along, or something like that) or to gain possession by wresting it from an opponent by brute force. As for rough play around the goals, eliminate it by placing the goals over the players' heads. (Who could get hurt jumping up and down under a goal?)

Sometime during the winter of 1890-1891, Dr. Naismith nailed up two peach baskets at opposite ends of the gymnasium, chose up sides, threw in a soccer ball, and basketball was born!

How did the dribble come into being?

The dribble was originally a defensive measure. When a player had possession of the ball and was so closely guarded that he could not pass it to one of his teammates, the only thing he could do was to lose possession voluntarily in such a way that he might possibly recover it. He accomplished this by rolling or bouncing the ball on the floor. In a short time, players realized that by bouncing the ball rapidly they could control it as well.

Dr. James A. Naismith, surrounded by players of the first basketball team.

During the Christmas vacation of 1891 some of the Springfield College students went home and began playing the game in their own local Y.M.C.A.'s. There were no rules in print at the time, so each student had his own particular version of the game.

It wasn't until January, 1892, that the rules of the game were published (in the school paper) under the heading, "A New Game."

The first set of printed rules signalled the rapid spread of basketball to all parts of the United States, Europe and South America. Soldiers introduced basketball in the Philippines in 1900, and the U.S. army of occupation taught the game to the Germans during World War I.

However, it wasn't until 1936 that basketball got its biggest boost when it was included in the Olympic Games at Berlin. Basketball had finally arrived as a major sport.

From then on, basketball — scholastic, collegiate and professional— grew even quicker than Topsy of *Uncle Tom's Cabin.*

An early college basketball game in Madison Square Garden.

One of the biggest boons to basketball's popularity was the staging of well-attended double-headers at New York City's Madison Square Garden. These games, more than any one thing, placed basketball in the big time. In addition, the intersectional games played at the Garden were of paramount importance in standardizing rule interpretations and introducing all styles of play to all parts of the nation.

The start of college basketball at Madison Square Garden was on December 29, 1934. Ask any basketball fan which teams played in that opening double-header and they will always recall two of them.

Has any college team won the NCAA Championship three consecutive years?

Lew Alcindor and his teammates at UCLA accomplished this hitherto unreached goal when they beat Purdue in the NCAA final in 1969. Previously, they had defeated North Carolina in the 1968 final and Dayton in 1967. Before we go into detail about Alcindor, let's take a look at the teams that won the NCAA back to back.

It occurred first in 1945 and 1946 when Oklahoma State, then known as Oklahoma A & M, turned the trick. Coach Henry Iba had a great basketball player named Bob Kurland—and it was with this young giant at the helm that Iba fashioned the first back-to-backer ever. Then along came the

(Left) Lew Alcindor scoring a field goal for U.C.L.A. against Santa Clara in the NCAA Western Regional title game. (Above) Alex Groza, basketball star of the 1948 and 1949 teams at Kentucky University.

Baron from Kentucky, Adolph Rupp. With such outstanding players as Ralph Beard and Alex Groza, the Wildcats put together two championships in 1948 and 1949.

Incidentally, it was in 1950 that the rarest of all twin wins was accomplished. That year City College of New York won both the NCAA and the NIT, the only time it has ever been done. To do it, Nat Holman's quintette beat Bradley University in the finals of both the NCAA and the NIT. A team now can no longer play in both tournaments, so that record can't be broken.

Getting back to the teams that have won NCAA titles back to back, after Kentucky it was another six years before the University of San Francisco performed the feat. Coach Phil Woolpert had one of the greatest teams ever put together, led by the legendary Bill Russell. It was five years later, in 1961, that the University of Cincinnati started its two-year stint. Coach Ed Jucker did not have a single superstar, but the Cincinnati basketball team was still able to win the biggest bauble. This, too, in spite of the fact that Ohio State had a superstar in Jerry Lucas. Meantime, on the Pacific Coast, Coach John Wooden was preparing his University of California (at Los Angeles) fans for the big one. In 1964, and then in 1965, with great performers like Walt Hazzard and Gail Goodrich, the Uclans won the NCAA twice in a row.

But the best was yet to come. With the arrival of Lew Alcindor, UCLA was so powerful that only twice did the Bruins go down to defeat. After a streak of 47 wins, they were upset by Houston, 71 to 69, when the "Big E," Elvin Hayes, outplayed Alcindor before an all-time record crowd of 52,693 at the Houston Astrodome. UCLA got revenge in the NCAA semi-finals, beating Houston, 101-69. The only other loss was to Southern California in their last regular season appearance before the NCAA championships in 1969. Alcindor accomplished what no other athlete had ever been able to do in leading his team to three straight crowns. Bill Russell had not been able to do it at San Francisco, Oscar Robertson had never ever been on a single winner, and the player that Alcindor has been compared to most, Wilt Chamberlain, could not lead his Kansas teammates to even one crown.

Who was basketball's first big man?

George Mikan, 6 feet 10 inches, 250 pounds, was the first of the truly great big men. His is an unusual story, in that Mikan was not much of a high school ball player. He tried getting into Notre Dame, but wasn't considered good enough to make it, so he turned to DePaul University, coached by a former Notre Dame star, Ray Meyers, and gained stardom. Meyers worked extended hours with Mikan and the combination of both their desires and energy produced a "superstar." And Mikan was just that. He was a college All-America in 1944, 1945 and 1946. Then he went on to professional basketball and completely dominated the sport. He was the reason that the Minneapolis Lakers (now the Los Angeles Lakers) were the kingpins. He spent ten years with the Lakers and was the first player

George Mikan hooking a shot in against Nat ("Sweetwater") Clifton of the New York Knicks.

to reach the 10,000-point scoring plateau. In Mikan's first seven seasons with the Lakers, Minneapolis won six championships. George was no graceful gazelle on the court. He was more like a stampeding elephant, dominating the backboards by sheer brute strength and power.

When it came time to pick the greatest player of the half-century, Mikan was the choice. He is the perfect example of what determination and desire can do. Of course, being 6 feet 10 inches tall and weighing 250 pounds doesn't hurt, either.

Who influenced defense more than any other player?

The answer here is Bill Russell. More than any one player, he dominated the sport by his superb defense. It's amazing that Big Bill would have to settle for being just an ordinary offensive ball player. But on defense he is a genius. There simply has never been a player of his size with his mobility, and quickness and anticipation. He would actually change the other team's offense. For one thing, any time a player from the opposition got past the backcourt men or the forwards and went driving for the hoop, there was Russell. That wasn't the end of it. If you passed off to a teammate, Russell could recover and switch to the man who had just been handed the ball. He terrorized players into changing the arc of their shots. And he gave his teammates the added capability of playing their men closer because they weren't afraid that the man might drive around them. If he did, Russell was always waiting. Since he came into the N.B.A. in 1956, Russell and his Boston Celtics have lost the N.B.A. championship only twice. In 1958, the St. Louis Hawks—with Bob Pettit, Clyde Lovellette and Cliff Hagan—beat Boston, but it should be pointed out that Russell was ill and out of several games. In 1967, "Wilt the Stilt" and the Philadelphia team tripped up the Celts. Other than that, the Boston entry has ruled the roost like no team in no other sport. And when he's asked why, the answer from Bill Russell is always the same: "You win with defense." You sure do, when that defense is someone named Bill Russell.

Who is "Wilt the Stilt"?

Every sport has one man about whom controversies wax hot and heavy. In basketball, it's Wilt Chamberlain. The reason is obvious, if you've ever seen Wilt. And how could you miss? At seven feet one inch and somewhere around 290 pounds, he's easily the strongest big man the game has ever known. If Mikan was like a stampeding elephant, then Wilt was like a herd of them, when the spirit moved him. The easiest way to get Wilt upset was to suggest that the spirit didn't always move him. Wilt, though, would have the kind of nights no one in the history of the sport could approach. There was, for example, a night in Hershey, Pennsylvania, when the Big Dipper decided to pour it on, and scored one hundred points against the New York Knicks. It's the record, of course, and even though it was set against a team that wasn't one of the strongest, bear in mind that Wilt holds the scoring record in every arena in the league. He didn't just pick the easy ones.

Bill Russell, player-coach of the Boston Celtics, brings his defensive prowess into play by blocking a shot by Keith Erickson of the Los Angeles Lakers in the final game of the 1969 N.B.A. championship play-offs. The Celtics went on to win another title.

His battles with Bill Russell are legends. That Russell could even give him a tussle is really a testimonial to Russell's tremendous winning desire. It's no secret that prior to some important games Russell has become sick to his stomach from anxiety. That's how intense a competitor he is.

No one knows for sure that Chamberlain doesn't get that intense, too. The fact is, he has always been so much stronger, faster, and taller than almost everyone he has played against that he has had too much going for him. He probably resented the fact that fans expected so much more from him. Then, too, there was always the embarrassment of the way he shot fouls. He just couldn't shoot fouls well, no matter what style he used. One-hand, two-hand, overhand, underhand, sidearm. Here was the basket, just fifteen feet away, with no one in the way, and all you had to do was put the ball in. Wilt couldn't. He's probably the only player ever with a better percentage from the field than the foul line.

And his life story has been a repeat story. He went to Kansas and everyone predicted that Kansas would win three championships. They didn't win even one. Well, you could excuse that by saying that he didn't have a good enough supporting cast. But the story was the same when he got to the pros. Added to his torment was his apparent inability to communicate with his coaches. They added to the enigma of a Gulliver-like tale. With all that height, all that speed, all that jumping ability, and all that incredible strength, how could he be tied down? It remains a mystery.

Versatile Oscar Robertson dribbles his way through the Boston Celtics toward the basket.

Who is the best all-around player?

Even old-timers agree about this one. The answer is the "Big O," Oscar Robertson. At six feet five inches he's not a little man, but in this day and age of the giants who play the sport, Oscar is just a little bigger than average. His skills with a basketball, though, are not just a little bigger than average—they are superior. Oscar has strength, speed, shooting touch, court sense, ball-handling skill, passing ability, defensive toughness, remarkable stamina, and alertness. There is not a trace of "showboat" in him. Everything he does is done so easily, you wonder how. He makes no Fancy-Dan passes. There's a simplicity to his game that makes you feel that almost anyone could do it. One of the strangest things about Oscar, though, is that, like Chamberlain, he never played on an NCAA championship team; and right after he left the University of Cincinnati, the Bearcats went on to two NCAA crowns. In the NBA, Oscar teamed with Jerry Lucas to give the pro Cincinnati Royals one of the most explosive one-two punches in the history of the game. It hasn't been good enough, though. There was always the specter of Bill Russell and the Boston Celtics.

What is the greatest scoring combination in the history of pro basketball?

Jerry West and Elgin Baylor of the Los Angeles Lakers. Jerry West is a coach's dream. From the time he made his debut on the national scene while with the West Virginia Mountaineers, West has been a prime example of the All-American boy—modest, retiring, never a harsh word about anyone, and always putting out on the basketball court. There have been many great shooters in this age of great shooters. No one could shoot it any better than Jerry. He's only a shade over six feet two, but he's really got spring in his legs. He can get up so high so quick that it's impossible to block his shot and he really goes to the hoop. No matter whether it's Bill Russell, or whoever, under that basket, West will go for the hoop, and most of the time it's good for two. In addition, West will give it everything he's got on defense. When West plays you, you've got to earn your points. If there was one phase of the game that wasn't quite up to the rest, it's the fact that Jerry's not a playmaker.

His teammate with the Lakers, Elgin Baylor, is probably the greatest offensive six-foot-five player in the history of the game. Baylor's body control is unmatched in basketball play. Watching him go up in the air and hang, or float, or just do anything, is worth the price of admission. Baylor learned the game in Washington, D.C. As a youngster, he used to practice by himself and he perfected all those incredible moves. Elgin comes to a man dribbling the ball, and then turns his back to the hoop, maneuvering, weaving and bobbing. Then, with that incredible "step" toward the basket, *bingo!* he scores two more.

Baylor originally was at the College of Idaho, but switched to Seattle University. There he turned the Chieftains into a power. You may not remember, though, that when Baylor came east to play in the N.I.T. he was not exactly sensational. Seattle played against St. Bonaventure, and the Brown Indians from Olean used a tactic that stunned the crowd. Instead of using one of their bigger players to guard Baylor, they gave the task to a six-foot-one guard named Brendan McCann, and it worked.

St. Bona upset Baylor and Seattle. After the game there were many in the crowd at Madison Square Garden who talked about how overrated Baylor was.

His first in the N.B.A. stopped all that talk. He wasn't good, or great. He was superstar material. Elgin averaged 34.9 points per game and despite being a small forward at 6′5″, he hauled down 1,050 rebounds. The Lakers jumped from last to second and beat St. Louis for the division title. It took the Boston Celtics to stop them.

Elgin Baylor of the Los Angeles Lakers jumps up to score against the St. Louis Hawks.

Jerry West of the Los Angeles Lakers.

Hank Luisetti, of Stanford University, the greatest basketball player of his time.

Which player started the basketball scoring revolution?

Angelo Enrico (Hank) Luisetti, born January 16, 1916 in the Telegraph Hill section of San Francisco, the same area which provided the New York Yankees with Joe DiMaggio, Frank Crosetti and Tony Lazzeri, is credited with giving basketball the same prominence Babe Ruth gave baseball and Red Grange, football. Before Luisetti came along, the game was a two-handed game. Occasionally someone would heave the ball at the basket with just one hand, but the instance was so rare and it brought forth such a quick "Cut that out!" from the coach that no one did it. Then Luisetti came east to Madison Square Garden to play against the best and to prove his claim to stardom. It was easy. Luisetti made the one-handed shot famous and basketball has never been the same since. Hank was tremendous at the Garden, but it was only the beginning. He moved on to Pittsburgh against a first-rate Duquesne team where he scored fifty points. That year he scored 305 points in eighteen games. It may not seem much by today's standards, but in those days it was the best.

There was only one other thing to add to the scoring punch. That last addition was the jump shot. There have been a lot of opinions on who originated the shot, but most people allow that it was Kenny Sailors, one-time Wyoming University star and later a stand-out in the pros, who

65

brought it into prominence. There are some who insist that John "Bud" Palmer, New York City's official greeter under Mayor John Lindsay, was one of the originals while playing for the New York Knickerbockers. One thing is certain, though. With the jump shot, the offensive player has had an advantage his predecessors never knew.

Who were the original Celtics?

This was a group of players which started as a semi-pro team in 1915. The Celtics dominated the American Basketball League formed in 1925 and one season won 109 out of 120 games. They were then thrown out of the league for being too strong. The Celtics put the show on the road and became bywords throughout the country. They would play about 150 games a year, winning 90 percent of them. At Cleveland, in 1922, they played before 23,000 spectators. They played in Madison Square Garden until the team was disbanded in 1928. The outstanding players on the Celtics included Joe Lapchick, Ernie Reich, Johnnie Beckman, Pete Barry, Chris Leonard, Dave Banks, George Haggerty, Elmer Ripley, Harry Brugge, Benny Borgman, "Stretch" Meehan, "Chief" Mueller, Jim Kane and two men who had enormous impact on the game, Nat Holman and "Dutch" Dehnert. It was Dehnert who was given credit for starting the "pivot" play in basketball. All he did was turn his back to the basket and set screens.

As for Holman, this incredible human was without peer in his own day as a ball player. He could run, pass and dribble superbly. His two-handed set shot was deadly. Nat went on after his playing days to become one of the great coaches of all time. It was his City College team of 1950 which won the NCAA and NIT in the same year. That hadn't ever happened before and probably won't again unless the rules are changed to allow a team to play in both tournaments. There is no relationship between the original Celtics and the Boston Celtics.

Who started the Harlem Globetrotters?

Abe Saperstein, a little man with a big dream, was the creator of the Harlem Globetrotters. It all started back in 1927 when Saperstein combined five players and an old automobile and started on the road.

The story of the Globetrotters has been told in a movie version, but the movies couldn't capture the whole flavor of it. Touring over millions of miles, the Globetrotters have been the greatest basketball ambassadors the game has ever known. Just name a place, whether it be Juneau, Alaska, or some spot in the arid area of the world, and they have been there. They have traveled by car, plane, ship, boat, horse and wagon—even by dogsled—and wherever they have played, they have delighted capacity crowds. They may not rank as one of the great playing teams, but their showmanship is incomparable. They have one purpose and one purpose only—to entertain the crowds. Who can forget Reece (Goose) Tatum, the man they called the Clown Prince of Basketball? With an arm span of 84 inches, the fact that he was only six feet three inches tall became meaningless. Goose did for children what Walt Disney did. He ran the gamut of their

Reece ("Goose") Tatum of the Harlem Globetrotters, putting on one of his typical clowning acts.

emotions and they loved him. Another outstanding player was Marques Haynes, a spectacular dribbler. Marques did everything with a basketball but eat it. When he dribbled the ball while on his knees with a speed and dexterity no one else could ever display, the crowd would "ooh" and "aah." Other key men included Ermer Robinson, Clarence Wilson, Josh Grider, William "Rookey" Brown and Sam Wheeler. These were the Harlem Globetrotters.

Which team holds the longest scholastic winning streak?

Coach Ernie Blood's Passaic (N.J.) wonder team ran up 159 consecutive victories before losing to Hackensack (N.J.), 39-35, on February 6, 1925. More recently, Power Memorial High School, with Lew Alcindor, ran off 71 straight before they ran into De Matha High School of Hyattsville, Maryland, which stopped the Power streak.

What is meant by a combination man-for-man zone?

This is about as good a time as any to go into defenses in basketball. There are differences in the pros where you cannot play a zone, although some of the teams hedge a little. But in amateur ball, you're allowed to use any defense. A man-for-man defense can be defined as one in which each defensive player is assigned a particular opponent, and during the rest of the game he sticks with him, no matter what. They tell the story of some players who would guard their assigned opponent from the time he came out of the dressing room.

Now, when a zone defense is in use, each player is stationed in a certain territory on the floor and is only responsible for the player in his territory or zone. In its simplest form, that's the difference between the man-for-man and the zone defense.

But there are too many in the business with enormous imagination for the game to have such simplistic form. At Notre Dame, one such man was the late great George Keogan. Recognizing the difficulties involved in straight man-for-man guarding, Coach Keogan used a "switching man-for-man." The basic concept here was that any time two offensive men crossed, instead of the defensive men doing the same, they would signal one another by yelling "switch." It was George Keogan who popularized this technique and helped the defense against the pressure of the screening and blocking plays the offense was using.

Later, Eddie Hickey, while coaching at St. Louis University with enormous success, added his own variations to the "switching" so that teams not only used lateral switches but also vertical. The result was that you couldn't tell the difference between Coach Hickey's defense and the zone defense. To add to the confusion, there were coaches like Joe Mullaney at Providence and Jack Kraft at Villanova who would combine and play you man-for-man on one side and zone on the other. This type of maneuvering was called a "Chinese" defense. It added to the woes of many teams. When watching a game, here's a way to determine what kind of defense a team is using. If a player on the offense runs toward the basket without the ball and is followed by one man, you can be pretty sure it's a man-for-man. Now, I admit that that makes it seem a little simpler than it sometimes is, but that's really the basis of it all. Today, most coaches will use that principle right at the start of a play. They'll just run a man through without the ball. If no one picks him up all the way, then they'll go into the zone offense.

What is the all-court press?

Actually, it's just what it sounds like. The defensive team picks you up from the time you take the ball out of bounds. Some teams used this strategy to slow you down in back-court while they set up a zone defense. Other teams use it to force you into a running game. That's the technique U.C.L.A. used so well against a bigger, stronger Michigan team that was also slower. When they got the Wolverines to run with them, they destroyed them. There's the man-for-man all-court press and the zone all-court press. The idea is the same as for the man-for-man and one that's played half-court. Just apply the same principles to full court and you've got it.

What are offensive formations?

Against a man-for-man defense, the standard is that if you've got a real big man, you get him as close to the basket as possible and let him put the ball in. This is where you hear the term "pivot man." That's the player with his back to the loop who keeps edging in close to the basket. If a team doesn't have that big man, you'll hear them say, "Keep the middle open." That simply means, "Give the smaller players a chance to use their speed and drive to go down the unclogged middle."

Once you get into operating against a zone, the formations are as many and varied as you can imagine. There's the three-two, the two-three, the two-one-two, the one-three-one, the two-two-one, and the three-one-one.

Obviously, it's impossible to capture the entire scope of basketball in just a few pages, but with these fundamentals, your idea of the game should be somewhat broader. The rest is up to you. Playing and viewing and reading extensively about the game will eventually get you your Ph.D.

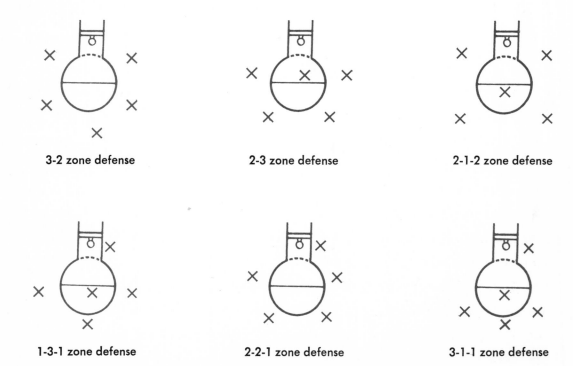

3-2 zone defense   2-3 zone defense   2-1-2 zone defense

1-3-1 zone defense   2-2-1 zone defense   3-1-1 zone defense

James J. Jeffries and
Bob Fitzsimmons in the ring.

Boxing

There is nothing that can arouse greater passions in men than boxing. You can get into a heated argument just by bringing up the subject and stating whether or not it should be abolished. Try it sometime. Just say to someone, "Boxing ought to be abolished." Get ready for a real argument. That's the nature of the "sport."

It has probably been that way since some ancient time when two men first got into a discussion that they couldn't settle with their mouths. "Oh, you think I'm wrong? . . . Well, put up your fists!"

You might suppose that because the word "pugilism" is derived from the Latin *pugil* (one who fights with his fists) it all began in ancient Rome. But Dr. E. A. Speiser and some of his associates have discovered slabs and figurines in a temple near Bagdad in Mesopotamia depicting men fighting with their fists prior to the time of the Romans and Greeks.

However, the Greeks really exploited boxing on a level that was unknown before them. When the Romans conquered Greece, they added their own refinements.

Boxing as we know it today has its roots in England (like baseball and football). The first recorded bouts took place over 250 years ago. James Figg is listed as the originator of bare-knuckle fighting. Figg was an excellent all-around athlete and he brought a new style to bare-knuckle fighting. Instead of wasting time trying to wrestle his opponents, as was the custom, he'd get in as close as he could, and when the other man tried to grab him, he'd just sock it to him. Since his opponents knew nothing about defense, Figg would have little trouble belting them. He either knocked them out or made them helpless.

He was an instant hit. Everyone talked about "Figg's Fighting." Figg became a teacher of the art of hitting a man on the chin. He retired as the undefeated champion. When he died, it was due to pneumonia.

After Figg's death, the next important figure in the sport was Jack Broughton. Broughton was considered (by the standards of his time) a great student of the sport. A public outcry to lessen the brutality of the sport prompted Broughton to draw up a set of fixed rules. He introduced them at a bout that took place on August 10, 1743.

While Figg ruled the roost, men had to continue fighting until there was a definite winner or loser; no rest periods were allowed. Broughton changed all that. His rules became known as the Broughton rules, and they governed boxing for many years. Then came the Marquis of Queensberry rules which were intended to keep boxing from being barbarous. There is still some question, even today, as to whether the Marquis succeeded. Much depends on the individual boxing fan. There are some who still "scream for blood," when they think the fighting is too tame.

In the early days in America, boxing was not viewed with favor. The first American champion was a gent named Jacob Hyer. All he had to do to win the crown was beat a man in a grudge fight—there was no one else really interested in challenging him. Twenty-four years later his son Tom announced that he had succeeded his father as champion. That was **that**.

John L. Sullivan

But news gets around fast, even when something is not viewed with favor. Some English fighters were soon battling here in the United States. Still, they drew only small crowds and made small news. Then along came a fighter named Paddy Ryan, who had had only four fights before meeting the English titleholder, Joe Goss. But Ryan beat Goss, and that made him world's champ. That still doesn't make it all sound too impressive. But then a fellow named John L. Sullivan appeared on the scene, and boxing now had its own Joe Namath. Sullivan was the man who brought boxing into focus. It got to the point where people were walking around saying, "Shake the hand that shook the hand of John L." That's how big John L. Sullivan was, and this was in a time even before radio. John L. was smart enough to know that he had to give the sport some "show biz." When he did, the sport took off like a moon rocket.

Who beat John L. Sullivan?

The man was James J. Corbett. "Gentleman Jim," they called him when he came into fame. He was from San Francisco, and he was the first boxer to "hit the big time." Sullivan, who had brought boxing from bare knuckles to gloves, was still just a brawler compared to this San Francisco dandy. Corbett boxed his ears off before knocking him out in the twenty-first round. They fought for a purse of $25,000 and a side bet of $10,000. Like Sullivan, Corbett subsequently embarked on a stage career. He was the more serious actor and starred in "Gentleman Jack," "The Cadet," and "Cashel Byron's Profession."

It took a most unlikely looking gent to knock off Gentleman Jim. He was "Ruby Bob" Fitzsimmons. Fitzsimmons not only won the heavyweight crown, but before he hung up his gloves he also won the middleweight and light heavyweight crowns. (He and Henry Armstrong are the only two fighters ever to win three different titles.) "Ruby Bob" was a string bean who could punch with unbelievable power. He fought until he was 52 years old (older even than Archie Moore). Fitzsimmons lost the heavyweight crown in his first defense of the title to one of the all-time great fighters, James J. Jeffries.

Who was known as the Boilermaker?

That's what they called James J. Jeffries. He was a brute of a man, and old-timers rank him as one of the very best. It was he who handled as murderous a puncher as Fitzsimmons with relative ease. He retired as the undefeated champion of the world in 1903. Then came one of the most controversial champions in the history of sports and Jeffries became unretired. That controversial champion was Jack Johnson. What made him controversial was that he was a black man. Feelings ran very high against Johnson, even though he was an outstanding fighter. Some authorities list him as the greatest heavyweight of them all. He was six feet one, and in

James J. Corbett—"Gentleman Jim"

James J. Jeffries—"The Boilermaker"

his prime he weighed anywhere from 205 to 220. Johnson was the son of a schoolhouse janitor and worked with his father until he took off on his own. He became a stable boy at a race track and did all kinds of odd jobs, including helping in the training of the original Joe Walcott. That got him started as a fighter and he kept going for some twenty years. Of all the so-called old-timers, Johnson's style is most like that of modern-day fighters. He was a stand-up boxer with great speed and hitting ability. In an age when there were many great Negro fighters, Johnson was the one who became the heavyweight champion.

He so dominated the division that there was a plea made to Jeffries to come out of retirement. The Boilermaker was way out of shape, but so strong was the pressure that Jeffries agreed to fight Johnson. It was a mistake. Jeffries was but a shell of the champion that he had been and Johnson beat him easily.

Jack Johnson at the time of his attempted comeback.

Jack Dempsey, the "Manassa Mauler," in training.

Who finally defeated Jack Johnson?

The Pottowotomie Giant, Jess Willard, finally accomplished what many considered the impossible. He knocked out Johnson in Havana, Cuba, in 26 rounds on April 5, 1915. It was one of the most debated fights of all time. A rumor was circulated that Johnson had taken a "dive," but Nat Fleischer, the great ring historian, disputes this and says that the contest was all on the up and up. Willard was the first real giant to fight in the ring with success. He was all of 6'6" and weighed around 250 pounds. He was a man of enormous courage, as many found out later when he fought the great Jack Dempsey.

Who was the "Manassa Mauler"?

The man who answered to that description was the one and only Jack Dempsey. There will always be arguments as to who was the greatest fighter of all time, but when fans talk about which one was best known for the longest time, the name of Jack Dempsey heads the list. There was no place on the face of the globe where people didn't know Jack. Even when he had been out of boxing for thirty years, an introduction of Dempsey would set a crowd into a roar of acclaim. It hadn't always been that way with Jack. After he had all but killed Jess Willard to win the title on July 4, 1919, Jack was roundly criticized because he had seen no service in World War I. Despite the fact that he had participated in some of the most sensational boxing contests of all time, such as the famed battle with the "Bull of the Pampas," Luis Firpo, Dempsey's status was always somewhat tarnished. Then came his battle for the heavyweight crown with Gene Tunney. Dempsey was beaten, and as so often happens when a man loses, he regained popular sentiment. And if he hadn't regained it at all, there was the return fight with Gene Tunney and the "long count" incident which made Jack Dempsey the most popular sports figure in the country. Everyone felt that Jack had gotten a "raw deal" from the referee who had allowed more than ten seconds to elapse before sending the two combatants back to fight. It had developed from the fact that in this fight they began the rule of making a man go to a neutral corner after a knockdown. Making Dempsey go to a neutral corner gave Gene Tunney precious time to get up—Tunney then went on to win.

Dempsey announced his retirement after the fight, but four years later he tried a comeback. This came to an end when "Kingfish" Levinsky won a decision over him.

Which fighter scored the most one-round knockouts in title fights?

Joe Louis was the most destructive exponent of the one-round knockout in title bouts. Louis scored ten of them in his career and five of these came in bouts with his title at stake. His quickest and most brutal was inflicted in 2 minutes 4 seconds the night he *blitzkrieged* Max Schmeling, an emissary out of Hitler's Germany who had gotten a telegram from the *Fuehrer* before the fight asking him to uphold the honor of the Master Race. It had to be the most satisfying experience of Louis' career. This fine young man, who had battled his way from the amateurs to the big time and had taken the world of boxing by storm with his ability and gentlemanly demeanor, had been badly battered in his first meeting with Schmeling. He had been knocked out in twelve rounds after taking a terrible beating. But getting knocked out in the ring was the least of it. Schmeling not only put him down in the ring but he "put him down" out of it. He belittled Louis both as a fighter and a man. The result was that the "Brown Bomber," as Louis was known, ached to get back at him, and when he finally got his chance, he more than evened the score.

How many heavyweight champions retired undefeated?

Technically, only four—James J. Jeffries, Gene Tunney, Joe Louis and Rocky Marciano. (Muhammad Ali did not retire.) Jeffries and Louis both

After losing to Max Schmeling in a previous bout, Joe Louis turned the tables in their second match, producing one of the quickest finishes to a world-heavyweight fight.

78

attempted comebacks and were unsuccessful. Gene Tunney is probably the most underrated fighter of all time. This ex-marine never captured the public fancy for a number of reasons. First of all, he read poetry, and that didn't sit too well with the fight public. And secondly, he beat Jack Dempsey. It made a hero of Dempsey and made Tunney even less popular. Actually, Gene was everything you'd want in a fighter. He could box, punch, and he had tremendous courage. His fights with Harry Greb are considered to be as viciously fought as any in the history of the game. Greb, in their first meeting, gave Tunney a fearful shellacking. A less courageous man would have quit the business. Gene not only didn't quit, but came back to beat Greb. When he hung up his gloves, Gene married into society — and that, along with the poetry, has made him seem outside the fold.

As for Rocky Marciano, they threw away the mold after they made him. He came out of Brockton, Massachusetts, and under the tutelage of Charlie Goldman, this 5'11" 185-pounder blockbusted his way to the championship. Marciano was strictly a made fighter. He was not what the fight crowd would call a natural. He did it all through sheer courage and hard work. No fighter ever worked harder than Marciano, who actually enjoyed training. It was this superb conditioning that stood him in such

Harry Greb

Gene Tunney taking the much-disputed "long count" in the famous title fight with Jack Dempsey.

good stead. He would come into the ring to fight and fight and fight. He'd hit you anywhere. In some of his fights he wore his opponents down by hitting them on the arms. Then he'd shift his target to the head and that was all there was to it. Like Dempsey, Marciano is a soft-spoken man. But his fists spoke loud and clear. He was never beaten as a professional. Forty-nine fights, forty-nine wins—forty-three of them by knockout.

The unbeaten heavyweight champion, Rocky Marciano.

Muhammed Ali, then known as Cassius Clay, after knocking down Sonny Liston in their second title bout.

Where does Muhammad Ali fit in?

I guess you'd have to say he fits in almost anywhere. As this is written, the story of this most controversial figure (of his or almost any other time) is out of boxing, but still in the limelight. With his great speed, probably the fastest heavyweight of them all, and size (six-feet three, 210 pounds), Ali had all the equipment save possibly one, a great knockout punch. But though he has had many detractors, there are none who now don't rate him as a great fighter. The funny thing is that almost every fighter who attained greatness always had detractors while he fought. When Marciano was champ, everyone said he was good, but not like Louis or Dempsey in their prime. When Louis was champ, they said that Dempsey or Jack Johnson would have taken him. There's always someone around talking about the "good old days" in all sports, not just boxing. But getting back to the subject of Muhammad Ali, all you can say is that he beat everyone they asked him to fight, and that's about all you can ask of any fighter.

Who were outstanding in the other divisions?

Besides the heavyweight division, the two others that have provided the most memorable champions are the lightweight and the middleweight classes. In the lightweight division, the first really great one was a fighter named Joe Gans. He was born Joseph Gaines on November 25, 1874, in Baltimore. He started as a pro in 1891 and finally got his chance for the world championship in 1900 against Frank Erne. It turned into a disappointment as Gans asked to have the fight stopped in the twelfth round because of an injury. However, two years later he got a rematch and knocked Erne out in one round. He was so good that he often fought outside of his own weight class. Once he fought the great welterweight champion, the original Joe Walcott, the "Barbados Demon," and the fight ended in a draw. He remained the lightweight champion for six years until he was knocked out by Battling Nelson in the seventeenth round on July 4, 1908.

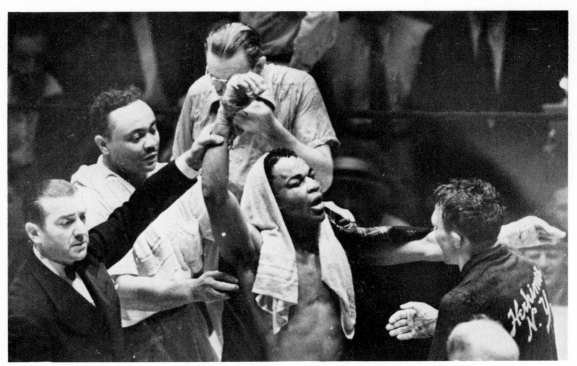

Henry Armstrong after he won his third world boxing title.

He lost again to Nelson and had one more fight before retiring in 1909. One year later, on August 10, 1910, he died of tuberculosis in Baltimore. In his almost twenty years in the ring, the record books credit him with fifty-five knockouts in 156 matches, of which he lost only eight.

And then there was Benny Leonard. Benny came out of the tough east side of New York, where one had to fight just to live. From 1917 to 1924 Benny dominated the lightweight division. That's not to say that he didn't have any tough fights. There was a night with Lew Tendler when Benny, after having been decked and out on his feet, talked his way out of trouble. "Is that the hardest you can hit?" Benny wanted to know. He got out of the jam and went on to win. Benny had all the tools of the trade—a great jab that he would hook off of, a marvelous right, and with all of that he was a boxing master. There are those who say that he was the greatest lightweight who ever laced on a pair of gloves. When he died, he died in the ring, refereeing a fight.

After Benny came some really good ones, the kind who deserve mention, like Tony Canzoneri and Barney Ross. They were outstanding. Both Tony and Barney were title-holders in other divisions. Barney also deserves mention as a hero of World War II.

But if you're ranking the superstars, the next one has to be Hammerin' Henry Armstrong. Armstrong, with the torso of a middleweight and the legs of a featherweight, came out of the West and left a record equalled by few. Everyone knows that he was a triple-crown winner. The only other man ever to do that was Bob Fitzsimmons. But did you know that in addition to winning the featherweight, lightweight and welterweight championships, Armstrong almost won the middleweight title from Ceferino Garcia? He fought Garcia, the middleweight champ, to a draw, and that's about as close as you can come. Hammerin' Henry was a perpetual motion machine—when he climbed into the ring he never stopped swinging. It sometimes looked as if he was trying to chase his opponent right out of the ring, and there were probably quite a few who wished that they had never gotten into the ring with him, once the bell rang.

They've run out of the Gans, Leonard and Armstrong molds. As a matter of fact, they don't make them like Tony Canzoneri or Barney Ross any more. What did you say? He sounds like an old-timer? O.K., then let's move to the middleweights. Can you think of some of the old-timers? How does the name Stanley Ketchell strike you? Remember how we talked about the great heavyweight, Jack Johnson? Would you believe that Stanley Ketchell not only fought Johnson but actually knocked him down? It was the last thing Ketchell did in that fight, because when Johnson got up, he knocked Ketchell out pronto. Ketchell was called the Michigan Assassin. He was a terrific hitter who began fighting when he was only sixteen years old. The string of knockouts that he piled up was so long it seems hard to believe. Finally, he got a crack at Mike (Twin) Sullivan for the middleweight crown—and the next thing you knew, Ketchell had knocked him out in one round. He kept going like that until Bill Papke stiffened him in twelve, but in a rematch Ketchell evened things up. There was one match, though, that Ketchell couldn't even up. A man named Walter Dipley shot him on October 15, 1910. It was fatal.

In discussing Gene Tunney, the name of Harry Greb came up. Whenever the ring fans talk of great fighters, that name always will. He was one of the greatest of them all. They nicknamed him "The Human Windmill" for an obvious reason—he was really tireless and fearless. He would fight anybody, including heavyweights. As a matter of fact, he wanted to fight Jack Dempsey, but the heavyweight champion said no, thank you. When you got Greb in the ring, it felt as if you were being towed under water. His fight with Mickey Walker is one they always mention when talk gets around to all-time fights. Their fight in the ring wasn't the end of it. They met on the street that same night and started all over again! It's a tribute to Mickey Walker's skill that he would take on Greb twice in one night.

You're probably wondering, "Is he ever going to mention Ray Robinson?" Well, the time has come. Let's start from the beginning. Ray Robinson's name is really Walker Smith. But no matter what you call him by name, when you talk about his fighting, you're talking about one of the greatest. Ring experts rate him the best pound-for-pound fighter of his time. He started as a lightweight, but the first title he won was the welterweight crown. Then he won the middleweight crown. Then he lost the middleweight crown. Then he won it. Then he lost it. Then he won it. In all, he won the middleweight championship *five* different times, and that's a record, not only for middleweights, but for all weights.

Ray almost became a triple-crown winner. He fought Joey Maxim for the light heavyweight championship and was leading by a tremendous

Sugar Ray Robinson regaining the middleweight crown against Carmen Basilio.

point-margin when he suffered heat prostration and couldn't come out for the fourteenth round. He wasn't the only one affected by the heat that night. The referee also collapsed. They could substitute for the referee, but when Robinson collapsed, no substitution was allowed and so Ray Robinson did not become a triple-crown champion. It was one of the fistic things that Robinson did not achieve.

What is the record for most knockdowns in one round?

The answer to this one brings us back to the Dempsey-Firpo fight, considered by many experts to have been the fiercest battle ever fought. It lasted two rounds, with Dempsey crushing the Wild Bull of the Pampas to the canvas seven times in the first three minutes. During those 180 seconds, Dempsey came within a whisker of losing his title when he was knocked out of the ring while a crowd of 90,000 at the Polo Grounds went into a wild uproar. In all, there were nine knockdowns in the first round. Firpo went down three more times in the second round as Dempsey, springing to the attack the instant the courageous Argentine rose, pummeled him savagely.

Jack Dempsey climbs back through the ropes after having been knocked through them by Luis Angel Firpo. In a dramatic follow-up, Dempsey went on to win this heavyweight-championship bout by a knockout.

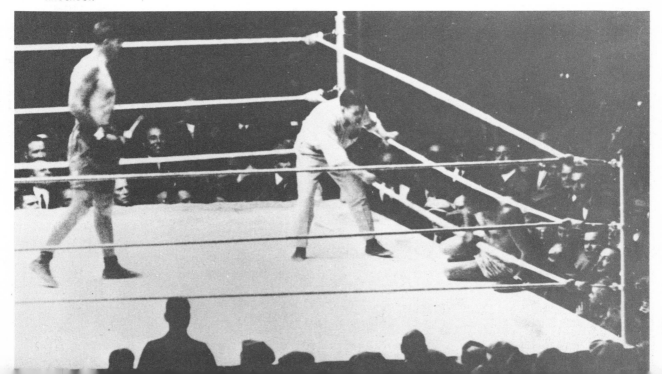

What is the record for most knockdowns in a fight?

Would you believe 49? It's hard to imagine two men having the stamina to last through so many knockdowns, but Battling Nelson, the great Danish lightweight champion, floored Christy Williams 42 times and hit the deck seven times himself before he put Williams away in the seventeenth round in a nontitle bout on December 26, 1902.

Williams shares the record for most knockdowns suffered by one fighter with Jack Havlin, who did the bouncing act over 29 rounds against Tommy Warren in San Francisco on September 25, 1888, when men were men. Warren never so much as smudged his trunks.

Which fighter holds the record for most knockouts?

Dapper, mustachioed Archie Moore, who had 226 bouts and won more than half of them—138—by knockouts. Moore started his career in 1936, but not until late in his career, in 1952, did he get a crack at a title, beating Joey Maxim for the light-heavyweight crown. He fought Rocky Marciano for the heavyweight title in 1955 and was knocked out in the ninth round. He retired in 1964.

A knockdown, while not always a prelude to a knockout, is a good measure of how soon a knockout might occur. Many fights have had many knockdowns, and in one real donnybrook, with both fighters hitting the canvas frequently, it was not the outcome that was in doubt, but which fighter would score a knockout first.

Archie Moore batters Yvonne Durelle of Canada en route to retaining the light-heavyweight title.

What was the longest glove fight on record?

Can you imagine two men belting each other for 110 rounds, a total of seven hours and 19 minutes, and nobody winning? That's what the two "gentlemen," Andy Bowen and Jack Burke, did on April 6, 1893, at New Orleans. The fight was called a draw by the referee when neither man could continue.

How are fights scored?

In different parts of the United States there are several ways of scoring a bout. In New York State, the referee and the judges score the fight on both a round-by-round and a point system. If a bout ends in a draw on the basis of rounds, then the officials revert to their point scores to determine a winner. The point system ranges from 1 to 4. A fighter's display of basic tactics is taken into account, and if he wins a round by a slim margin he gets a point, the loser zero; a decisive round will earn two points; a one-sided round or one in which a knockdown has been scored will earn three points; and a one-sided round with two or more knockdowns, four points.

In most states affiliated with the National Boxing Association, the five-point must system is the rule. That is, a fighter winning a round, even if only by a shade, will get five points. A knockdown and a clear superiority in a round will give the winner a 5-to-3 margin, and so forth. In a similar way a ten-point must system is used in Massachusetts, Ohio, Texas, and Miami Beach.

New Jersey uses a rounds system (no points). In California a five-point system is in effect, but the winner can receive anywhere from one to five points, the loser zero. It's not uncommon for a round to be scored 0-0.

As you can see, there's a lot to be said for the knockout. It does away with all that arithmetic, it settles the issue once and for all, and there is something infinitely satisfying in seeing someone twice as big as you stretched out on the canvas.

Here are some fast questions and answers to challenge you.

What was the largest live gate in boxing history?

The second Dempsey-Tunney fight at Soldiers Field, Chicago. The gate was $2,658,660! And remember, there was no TV money in those days! The time was 1927.

What was the largest live attendance at a fight?

The first Dempsey-Tunney fight at Sesqui-Centennial Stadium, Philadelphia, September 23, 1926. The attendance was 120,757. On August 18, 1941, Tony Zale and Billy Pryor fought before 135,132 in Milwaukee, at the Fraternal Order of Eagles Free Show.

How many fighters have never been defeated in a pro career?

Four, Rocky Marciano (1947-1955), 49 fights; Jack McAuliffe (1884-1897), 53 bouts; Larry Foley (1886-1888), 22 fights; Jimmy Barry (1891-1899), 70 bouts.

Who refereed the most title bouts?

Yes, referees set records, too. Arthur Donovan refereed fourteen title fights in the boxing ring.

Who was the youngest fighter to win a heavyweight title?

Floyd Patterson, at 21, was the youngest fighter to win a heavyweight title. Two other youngsters who did it were Cassius Clay (22) and Joe Louis (23). Jersey Joe Walcott was the oldest, at 37.

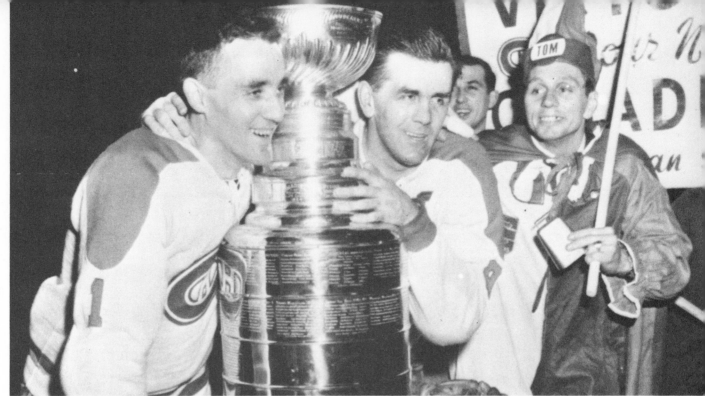

Jacques Plante (left) and Maurice ("Rocket") Richard pose with the coveted Stanley Cup, emblematic of world hockey supremacy.

Hockey

If you're under the impression that only in the United States do they debate origins of sports, rest easy. The quickest way to get two Canadians into a debate is to ask, "Where did hockey get started?" I said quickest, but I should have added that it ought to be a Canadian from Western Canada and one from Eastern Canada.

When the governing officials of hockey decided that a Hall of Fame was needed, their plan for getting a site was based on giving it to that community which could best show that it indeed was the birthplace of the game. Three very strong bids were made by Montreal, Kingston and Halifax. The Canadian Amateur Hockey Association then appointed a committee to render a decision. They came to the conclusion that Kingston, Ontario had the strongest claim. The committee traced the game in Kingston back to 1855. The first players were members of Her Majesty's Royal Canadian Rifles. There were some who made an even prior claim to the game's having been played as early as the 1830's.

Montreal did not take to the decision without some rancor. Those who opted for Montreal claimed that the first true game of ice hockey was played in Montreal in 1875 by teams of students from McGill University. But there were complications here, because if you accepted the story that students at McGill had started the game, then there seemed some evidence that one of those students, J. G. A. Creighton, had brought it to the campus from his home town of Halifax. And that's where it stood.

Then National Hockey League officials approached the leaders of the Canadian National Exhibition in Toronto, where Canada's Sports Hall of Fame had been established, and that's where the Hockey Hall of Fame was installed.

Which was the first hockey league?

As you might expect, the first hockey league revolved around Kingston. There were four teams in the league established at Kingston in 1885 —the Royal Military College, Queen's University, the Kingston Athletics and the Kingston Hockey Club. The Queen's University players were the first champions.

Which came first, the National Hockey League or the Stanley Cup?

The Stanley Cup. That may seem strange to those who have the impression that first came the National Hockey League and then came the Stanley Cup. It's just the other way around. The Stanley Cup preceded the National Hockey League by quite a few years. It was first presented to the team winning the championship of Canada in 1893. The National Hockey League came into existence in 1917. So there's a time span of 24 years. The Stanley Cup came into being as a result of the interest not of Lord Stanley, the Governor General, but of his aide, Lord Kilcoursie. It seems that Lord Kilcoursie had become quite a hockey enthusiast, and at his suggestion Lord Stanley of Preston donated the prize. The first winner was the Montreal A.A.A. team.

Which were the first teams in the N.H.L.?

The National Hockey League, an outgrowth of the National Hockey Association, was organized November 22, 1917, in Montreal. It was composed of the Montreal Canadiens, the Montreal Wanderers, Ottawa, Quebec, and the Toronto Arenas. Quebec did not operate that season. Later in 1918, when the Westmount Arena, home of the Wanderers, burned, the team dropped out of existence.

Which was the first United States team?

In 1924, the Boston Bruins became the first United States team. Then the New York Americans came into the league, followed by the Pittsburgh Pirates, both in 1925. In 1926, the New York Rangers, the Chicago Black Hawks and the Detroit Cougars were admitted.

What is so special about June 5, 1967?

That's the day the National Hockey League expanded from a six- to a twelve-team league. The Eastern Division consisted of the older teams: the Montreal Canadiens, the Toronto Maple Leafs, the Boston Bruins, the New York Rangers, the Chicago Black Hawks, and the Detroit Red Wings (the Cougars of old).

The new Western Division shaped up this way: the Los Angeles Kings, the Minnesota North Stars, the Oakland Seals, the Philadelphia Flyers, the Pittsburgh Penguins, and the St. Louis Blues.

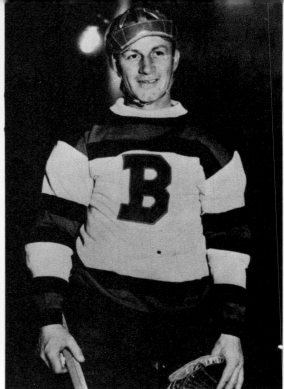

Bill Chadwick (right), hockey's most famous referee, with Clarence Campbell, president of the National Hockey League.

Eddie Shore

What is the Hart Memorial Trophy?

This is an annual award made to the player adjudged to be most valuable to his team. The winner is selected in a poll of the National Hockey League Writers' Association in the twelve N.H.L. cities at the end of the regular schedule. The winner receives $1,500 and the runner-up gets $750.

The Hart Memorial Trophy was presented by the National Hockey League in 1960 after the original Hart Trophy was retired to the Hockey Hall of Fame. The original Hart Trophy was donated to the N.H.L. in 1923 by Dr. David A. Hart, father of Cecil Hart, the former manager-coach of the Montreal Canadiens. The first winner was Frank Nighbor of the Ottawa team. Gordie Howe, the fabulous Detroit Red Wing, has won this award more times than any other player—six times he has been chosen as most valuable player in the league. Eddie Shore, another great of another period, was given the award on four different occasions. Howe, Shore, the late great Howie Morenz, and the two Chicago Black Hawk superstars, Bobby Hull and Stan Mikita, have taken the trophy in back-to-back years.

What is the Clarence S. Campbell award?

The Clarence S. Campbell Bowl is presented each year to the team finishing first in the Western Division at the end of the regular championship schedule. Accompanying the trophy is a monetary award totaling $47,250, based on 21 units of $2,250 each.

This award is presented by the member clubs for perpetual competition by the National Hockey League in recognition of the services of Clarence S. Campbell, who was named president of the N.H.L. in 1946 and still holds that position.

What is the Prince of Wales Trophy?

The Prince of Wales Trophy is presented each year to the team finishing in first place in the Eastern Division at the end of the regular championship schedule. Accompanying the trophy is a monetary award totaling $47,250, based on 21 units of $2,250 each. The Prince of Wales donated the trophy to the National Hockey league in 1924. From 1927-28 to 1937-38 the award was presented to the team finishing first in the American Division of the N.H.L. From 1938-39 (when the N.H.L. reverted to one section) to 1966-67, it was presented to the team winning the N.H.L. championship. With the expansion in 1967-68, it again became a divisional trophy.

What is the Art Ross Trophy?

This is an annual award to the player who leads the league in scoring points at the end of the regular season. The overall winner receives $1,000 and the overall runner-up $500. The leader at the end of the first half of the season and the leader of the second half each receive $500. The runners-up in each half get $250.

This award was presented to the National Hockey League in 1947 by Arthur Howie Ross, the former manager-coach of the Boston Bruins. If two players finish the season with the same number of points, the Trophy is awarded to the player with the most goals. If they have the same number of goals, then the player having played fewer games gets it. If they've played the same number of games, then it's the one who scored first during the season.

The first scoring leader was Joe Malone of the Montreal Canadiens in 1918. The man who has won this award the most times is the same player who has won the Hart Trophy most, Gordie Howe. Six times the big forward has outscored everyone in the league. In recent times, though, the Ross Trophy has been the personal property of those two Chicago Black Hawk scorers, Bobby Hull and Stan Mikita. From 1960 to 1968, Mikita led the league four times and Hull three. However, it remained for a member of the Boston Bruins to make the most indelible mark in the world of hockey that anyone had produced up to 1969. That Boston Bruin, Phil Esposito, became the first man ever to score more than a hundred points in a season. (The record had been 97 points, held jointly by Hull and Mikita.) Esposito tallied the almost unbelievable mark of 126 points. He didn't break the record—he destroyed it! En route he brought two others over the one-hundred mark, Bobby Hull and the seemingly never-ending Gordie Howe. Hull scored a total of 58 goals to break his own mark of 54. Even that wasn't the end of the record outpouring of scoring. The young great defenseman of the Boston Bruins, Bobby Orr, scored 21 goals to break the old mark of 20 held by Flash Hollett of the Detroit Red Wings that had been set in 1944-45. Orr also set the record for most points in a season by a defenseman, 64.

What other scoring record fell in 1968-69?

The 1968-69 season was the all-time season for record-breaking. In addition to most points (126) by Phil Esposito of Boston, most goals (58) by Bobby Hull, most goals by a defenseman (21), and most points by a

Bobby Orr

Frank Mahovlich

defenseman (64), both by Bobby Orr, there were many others. Pat Stapleton of the Chicago Black Hawks had the most assists ever by a defenseman. His total of 50 broke the previous mark of 46 held by Bill Gadsby while at New York and Pierre Pilote while at Chicago. Phil Esposito, on his way to 126, broke the record for most goals in a season by a center. His total of 49 was better than the old total of 47 by Jean Beliveau of the Montreal Canadiens. Esposito also set an all-time mark for most assists in a season at 77. Stan Mikita had had the old assists record of 62 in a season.

Two rookies, Danny Grant of Minnesota and Norm Ferguson of Oakland, set the new standard for most goals by a new man. They both had 34, which was four better than what Bernie ("Boom-Boom") Geoffrion had done for Montreal in his first year.

But there was even more of this hectic pace. The Boston Bruin line of Phil Esposito, Ken Hodge and Ron Murphy totaled 263 points, and that sent the 226 total by Detroit's Norm Ullman, Gordie Howe and Ted Lindsay into oblivion. Howe, though, combined with Alex Delvechio and Frank Mahovlich for 114 goals, and that one-season mark erased the old one of 105 set by the great Montreal line of Maurice ("Rocket") Richard, Elmer Lach and Hector ("Toe") Blake.

What is the Calder Trophy?

This is an annual award to the player selected as the most proficient in his first year of competition in the N.H.L. The winner is selected in a poll of the N.H.L. Writers' Association in the twelve N.H.L. cities at the end of the regular schedule. The winner receives $1,500 and the runner-up $750. The trophy is given in memory of Frank Calder, a former president of the N.H.L. Mr. Calder had originated the award, and the league perpetuated the trophy after his death. To be eligible for the award, a player cannot have played more than 25 games in any single previous season or in six or more games in each of any two preceding seasons. The list of winners of this particular award is an impressive one, although probably if one were to pick the most significant year, it would be 1958, when Frank Mahovlich just beat out Bobby Hull.

What is the James Norris Memorial Trophy?

This award is given annually to the defenseman who demonstrates throughout the season the greatest all-around ability in that position. The winner is selected in a poll of the N.H.L. Writers' Association. The winner gets $1,500 and the runner-up $750. The award is made in memory of the late James Norris, former owner-president of the Detroit Red Wings.

This is the newest of the N.H.L. achievement awards, having first been presented in 1953. Since that time, it has been practically the personal property of Doug Harvey, one of hockey's all-time greats. Harvey has won this award seven times. Pierre Pilote was able to capture the trophy on three occasions, and it seems now that the great young Boston Bruin, Bobby Orr, will come close to the Harvey mark if his legs hold out. Orr is perhaps the most exciting defenseman in the history of the game. He certainly is the greatest "offensive" defenseman the game has produced. Orr has tremendous speed and is one of the game's greatest shooters. It is almost beyond belief that one so young could be so great. Bobby has been playing with the "big boys" since he was fourteen and he has more than held his own.

Doug Harvey

Jacques Plante ready to stop a goal.

What is the Vezina Trophy?

This award is given annually to the goalkeeper or goalkeepers for the team with the fewest goals scored against it. The overall winner receives $1,500 and the runner-up $750. The leaders at the end of the first and second halves of the season, respectively, receive $250.

Leo Dandurand, Louis Letourneau, and Joe Cattarinich, former owners of the Montreal Canadiens, presented this award in memory of Georges Vezina, the great goal tender of the Canadians who collapsed during an N.H.L. game and died a few months later. He had contracted tuberculosis. Winners of this award read like a "Who's Who" of goal tending. For some years two men held the record for having won the award most times at six. Those two, both members of the Montreal Canadiens, were Jacques Plante and Bill Durnan. During the 1968-69 season, Plante, now in the uniform of the St. Louis Blues, combined with another all-time great, Glenn Hall, to win the Vezina Trophy. For Plante it was a historic seventh time that he had achieved the distinction and he had come out of retirement to join the Blues. He and Hall also were the first goal tenders of an expansion team to win this trophy.

Which team has won the Prince of Wales Trophy most?

Since this is an older award than the Clarence S. Campbell award, there's a longer period for one team to operate. So it is that the Montreal Canadiens, after the 1968-69 season, had won it eighteen times. In winning the trophy for the eighteenth time, the Canadiens set a record for most wins in one season, 46, and most points in a season, 103. They did it all for a rookie coach, Claude Ruel, who had succeeded the great Toe Blake as coach of the Canadiens. Ruel had been a player in the Canadiens organization until he was injured and lost the sight of an eye. It was after this injury that Ruel became a coach . . . and his success is obvious.

What is the Lady Byng Trophy?

There is something most unique about this award. Hockey is considered by some to be the roughest sport played. The Lady Byng Trophy is given to the player who is adjudged to have exhibited the best type of sportsmanship and gentlemanly conduct combined with a high standard of playing ability. The winner of the award, chosen by the N.H.L. Writers' Association, gets $1,500 and the runner-up $750.

This award was first presented in 1925 by Lady Byng, the wife of Canada's Governor-General at the time. After Frank Boucher of the New York Rangers won the award seven times in eight seasons, he was given the trophy to keep and Lady Byng donated another trophy. Boucher, who was the center for the great Ranger line that included the immortal Cook brothers, Bill and Bun, is the player most associated with this particular award. What is interesting is that in recent years a player as aggressive as Stan Mikita of the Chicago Black Hawks has been able to win the award. There are some players, of course, to whom this award is of no great consequence. Gordie Howe, perhaps the greatest all-around player of all time, has always said that this trophy held no great fascination for him.

What is the Conn Smythe Trophy?

This is the newest of the player awards and is presented to the most valuable player in the Stanley Cup play-offs. The winner is selected by a vote of the league governors at the conclusion of the final game of the Stanley Cup play-offs. Each governor files one ballot with the president, indicating his choice, in order of preference, with values of five, three or one for each choice. The winner gets $1,500.

The award was presented in 1964 by Maple Leaf Gardens, Limited, to honor Conn Smythe, former coach, manager, president, and owner-governor of the Toronto Maple Leafs.

Who is hockey's greatest player?

Just as in any other sport, any one player you pick as the "greatest" will get you into a debate. It would seem that in this sport the choice of greatest would be easier than in any other. Let's look at it this way. If you're going to pick the greatest, what would be the yardstick? You'd think in terms of offense and defense, plus length of service. When those measurements are used, the answer really is pretty obvious. The name of the player has to be Gordie Howe. He's the greatest scorer in the history of the game. He has been playing so long now that it seems he has always been around, doing it all. He can play offense, defense, anywhere. Add to that the fact that in as rough and tough a sport as hockey, he's as rough and tough as they come. Just look at the record. Through the 1968-69 season, Howe had played for 23 years. In that time he has scored the most points, the most goals, won the Hart and Ross trophies more than anyone, and has become one of the three players to break the 100-point mark.

But just looking at statistics, while they are very indicative of what Gordie Howe has done, still doesn't tell the whole story. You have to see the man in action. Tall, slope-shouldered, strong, a marvelous skater, a fearless competitor, a great passer, a right-handed or left-handed shooter,

Gordie Howe scoring the five-hundredth goal of his career.

and with an almost unbelievable third sense, Howe does it all. The great goal tender, Jacques Plante, was once asked whom he considered the greatest player of all. He answered immediately, "Gordie Howe." And Plante had played with the great "Rocket" Richard. But in comparing the two, Plante was quick to point out that while he did not think Howe was necessarily a greater scoring threat than Richard, Gordie just did *more* things on the ice. If Howe has ever seemed to lack any quality, it's probably because he has never been a colorful player. Gordie does it with such ease that it seems as if anyone could do it. He is the perfect "pro."

Who was the most exciting hockey player?

Two players stand out above the rest: the great Maurice ("Rocket") Richard of the Montreal Canadiens, and the "Golden Jet," Bobby Hull of the Chicago Black Hawks.

For eighteen seasons, Joseph Henri Maurice Richard, better known as the "Rocket," put on his twelve pounds of shin and shoulder pads, ankle-length underwear, skates, and stovepipe pants to maintain his position as the most exciting player around. He was a demigod to his rabid French-Canadian followers, a king, the goal-scoring nonpareil, the most dynamic and dramatic star in professional hockey. Richard scored his final goal for the Montreal Canadiens in the 1960 Stanley Cup play-offs. It was his 82nd in Stanley Cup play, a record, and it raised his lifetime total to 626.

On November 9, 1952, when the Rocket tallied his 325th goal, he became the National Hockey League's highest individual scorer in history. The puck was sent to Queen Elizabeth of England.

Richard had a fiery temper that caused many a rhubarb around the league. A stiff penalty imposed on Richard prompted the infamous Montreal riot of March 17, 1955, wherein unhappy fans capsized street-cars, broke store windows, and pelted the league president with assorted rancid grocery articles. Only an impassioned plea by Richard himself on radio and TV quieted them.

Richard was strictly a one-way player. The arrow always pointed toward the other team's goalie. He once scored five goals and three assists in a game.

But the best indication of this man's attitude can be seen in a story told by hockey referee Bill Chadwick. Years after Chadwick had retired from the game he asked Richard for an autograph for his son. "Why should I give it to you?" asked Richard. "All you ever did for me was give me penalties!"

That's not the case for Robert Marvin Hull. There never was or will be a hockey player more conscious of what he considered his responsibility to the public than the "Golden Jet." Bobby Hull has a quality that is associated with Babe Ruth. The fans everywhere love him and he loves them. He would no sooner pass up a fan looking for his autograph than pass up an opportunity to put the puck in the net for his team.

The greatest single-season goal-scorer in the history of the sport is that kind of man. And everything about him tells you that he's enjoying him-

Maurice ("Rocket") Richard

self. He loves to play and he loves to smile. Those who are critical of Bobby Hull say that if he were a meaner player, he'd be greater. When you tell that to Bobby, he laughs and says, "I'm trying to beat them, not kill them." The sight of Hull coming down the ice at full speed, though, is quite enough to strike fear in the heart of a goalie. When Bobby lets that 120-mile-an-hour shot go, it's a blur!

He is the only player in the game who through the 1968-69 season has scored fifty or more goals in four different seasons. His total of 58 in the 1968-69 season is a record, and an incredible one when you realize that he played a good portion of it with a broken jaw that had to be wired. It made eating very difficult, and when you can't eat, you're not quite as strong. But even below normal strength, Hull is a marvel.

At 5'10", 198 pounds, with the arms of a Neanderthal man and the torso of a weightlifter, Hull on skates is a sight to behold. Like all great athletes, Bobby has great balance. With that great strength and that great balance and the great shot he has, the wonder is that Hull hasn't passed the 60-goal mark for a season. He may still do it.

One thing he has done for the sport goes beyond his playing skill. He has been a great representative to the young off the ice—and in the long run, that may be his greatest contribution.

What is unusual about Bill Chadwick?

Bill Chadwick may be the greatest referee the sport of hockey has ever had. In a sport dominated by Canadians, Bill Chadwick is unusual in that he is from the United States. But even that doesn't tell the whole story. What is most unusual about Bill Chadwick is that while he was an active official, he had only partial sight. As a youngster, while playing hockey in his native New York City, Bill was the victim of an accident that robbed him of practically all vision in one eye. Despite this handicap, Chadwick, with the sanction of the governors of the National Hockey League, worked and became a great hockey official.

What was the origin of hockey in the United States?

In 1893, two Yale tennis champions, Malcolm G. Chace and Arthur E. Foote, started the sport on the New Haven campus. The game quickly spread throughout the nation. Three years later the Amateur Hockey League was formed in New York and a league was started in Baltimore. The rise of the professional game stimulated amateur interest. Presently there are more than three hundred teams, including many in the N.C.A.A., registered with the Amateur Hockey Association.

Ice hockey first became part of the Olympic schedule in the 1929 games in Amsterdam. Canada, because of its experience in the sport, emerged with the gold medals in 1920, 1924, 1928 and 1932. The British broke the string in 1936. The United States won the championship once, in 1960.

Can U.S. teams become National Hockey League players?

The expansion of the National Hockey League has probably given hockey a greater impetus in the United States than anything else that's happened in a long time. With teams located in six more cities in the United States, the youngsters get a chance to see more of the game. And with the games being televised nationally, more young people are exposed to it. All of these factors will help toward getting more youngsters skating, and that's the one really big thing in getting any sport started in a big way. There are, of course, quite a few areas which have been "hotbeds of hockey" in the United States. In Minnesota, for example, high schools play a state tournament which has an extremely popular following. The New York City area has had a rebirth of interest. What is needed now is for more of these young people to get enough competition so that they can play college hockey, and then the likelihood is that there will be plenty of U.S. teams playing the game in the National Hockey League.

This National Hockey League game was won by the Montreal Canadiens whose goalie, Jacques Plante, is shown here successfully fending off a shot attempted by the New York Rangers.

Francis Ouimet shaking hands with Harry Vardon (left) and Ted Ray (right), his opponents in the 1913 U.S. Open Golf Championship. Ouimet scored one of the game's biggest upsets by winning.

Golf

You can have more fun talking about the beginnings of the game of golf than about any other sport. Somewhere, someone wrote that Adam actually was the first golfer. It seems that he made a club from one of his ribs—and Eve thus became the first golf widow.

There is the group that always refers to horse racing as the sport of kings. You could get a good argument from golf historians who will say that royalty has indulged in golf, too. And quite a few notables of history were addicted to the pursuit of the little ball around green pastures. Some historians seriously claim that shepherds tending flocks of sheep in ancient times were the first to apply a stick to a ball, or more accurately, a club to the ball.

But there seems little doubt that the game as we know it today was first played by the Scots. Golf is known to have been popular around 1440, so popular that James II took a dislike to what the people were doing and prevailed upon Parliament to enact a rule during the month of March making it unlawful to play the game.

Then along came James IV, and he took enough of a liking to the game to indulge in it himself, becoming a fair player. His son, James V, didn't play, but neither did he stop anyone.

The first lady golfer was apparently Mary, Queen of Scots. With her appearance on the links the game took a real stride forward. It was during her reign (about 1552) that St. Andrews, the most famous of golf clubs, was founded.

Apparently, there were no Ben Hogans, Arnold Palmers or players of that calibre at that time, because there are no reports about them. If there were any great players, they played in private. But that seems impossible. Have you ever heard of a silent golfer? Come to think of it, I've heard of one named Willie Anderson. More about Willie Anderson later.

When did the British Open start?

In 1860, a tournament was held at the Prestwick Club in Scotland which was the beginning of the British Open. Willie Park, Sr. and Tom Morris, Sr. dominated the game. Between them they won the first five tournaments; Morris won three times and Park twice.

Tom Morris, Jr. won in 1868, 1869 and 1870. Then there was a halt in playing for several years. It didn't have any effect on Morris, because when playing resumed in 1872, this young man, a truly fine player, again won the title. In a time when the gutta-percha ball was played, Tom Morris, Jr. shot a 149 for 36 holes. No one ever shot better with the solid gutta-percha ball.

As for the beginnings of the game in North America, there are mentions of golf clubs having existed in South Carolina and Georgia during the eighteenth century, but there is no record of play. Some historians say that Scottish regiments stationed there were the first to play the game.

The game as we now know it was first played in the 1880's, however. A gentleman named Joseph Mickle Fox, a Philadelphian, learned about the game on a trip to Scotland, and when he returned he introduced it at his summer home. This led to the founding of the Foxburg Golf Club in 1887. That would make the club about the oldest in the United States.

When did the U.S. Open start?

It was started in 1894 at a course known as St. Andrews Golf Club in Yonkers, N. Y., which seems like poetic justice. The Yonkers club came into being as a result of the work of John Reid, who has been credited as the father of American golf. Mr. Reid was a transplanted Scotsman, and it was at a dinner party given for a group of his friends that the St. Andrews Golf Club was conceived. It was on that course in 1894 that Willie Dunn defeated Willie Campbell two-up to win the first U.S. Open.

When was the United States Golf Association formed?

In the same year that the first U.S. Open was played, the U.S. Golf Association was born. Clubmen decided that an official organization was needed and that rules should be set forth, including stipulations regarding amateurs and pros in the sport. And so was born the U.S.G.A.

When was the first amateur championship played?

This event took place in 1895, and the first United States amateur champion was a gentleman named C. B. MacDonald. Mr. MacDonald beat C. E. Sands by the comfortable margin of 12 and 11 (12 holes up with 11 to play). The next day they played the U.S. Open on the same course at Newport. This time it was medal play instead of match play. In medal play you just count strokes, while in match play you play hole by hole. When Willie Dunn had won the first open in 1894, it was match play. This time, at medal play, the winner, Horace Rawlins, shot 173 for 36 holes.

When did the ladies start their championship?

Women had taken an interest in the game from the time that it was introduced in Yonkers, and so when the men said they were going to have an amateur championship, the ladies decided they wanted one, too. The U.S.G.A. women's amateur championship came into being in 1895. There were thirteen contestants at the new Meadow Brook Club course on Long Island to determine a women's champion. It was medal play and Mrs. C. S. Brown was the winner with a total of 132 shots for 18 holes—not exactly inspiring. The next year it was changed to match play, and it has stayed that way since. Just like the ladies—they did it opposite to what the men had done in the Open.

Who was Willie Anderson?

This man is one of the men of mystery of any sport. Would you believe that Willie Anderson won the U.S. Open *four* different times? Yet, very few people have even heard of him. As a matter of fact, even the people of his time took little notice of him, as strange as that may seem. Here's a man who wins four U.S. Opens and very little is known of where he was from, how he got into the game, or how he came to this country. Talk about the Silent Scot. There apparently was no more Silent Scot than Willie Anderson. But silent or not, this gentleman won the U.S. Open in 1901. He didn't repeat in 1902, but he more than made up for that by coming back to win in 1903, 1904 and 1905, three years in a row. No one in the history of golf ever was able to win three U.S. Opens in a row. No one. Only two other golfers were able to win four U.S. crowns—Ben Hogan and Bobby Jones. More about them later.

Who were Vardon and Ray?

It sounds like the name of a cough drop unless you really know your golf. If you do, then you know that Harry Vardon and Ted Ray were two players from England who made a terrific impact on the game in the United

States. Harry Vardon made the more lasting one because it was his grip on the golf club, the Vardon grip, which is the most popular golf grip known. They tell the story that Vardon's greatest difficulty in playing the game was that the second day he played on a golf course, he would be hitting the ball out of his own divots. You all know, of course, that a divot is a bit of turf knocked out of the ground by the club when you hit a golf shot. After the shot, the turf is replaced. Vardon won the British championship six times and the American title once. As for his compatriot, Ted Ray, he was a brute of a player who knocked the cover off the ball with every swing; and when one mentions divots, the ones that Ray took were the size of throw rugs. These two men played the game in an opposite manner. Ray was the home-run hitter, Vardon was the stylist.

What young American beat Vardon and Ray?

There was one player in it who had grown up right across the way from the Country Club. His name was Francis Ouimet. If you had ever breathed his name in the same company as Harry Vardon and Ted Ray, knowledgeable golfers would have thought you were out of your mind.

So it was that at the end of the first 36 holes of play, Vardon and another Englishman, a fellow named Reid, were tied at 147. Ted Ray was two shots behind. At 151 was twenty-year-old Francis Ouimet, and he was tied with another twenty-year-old by the name of Walter Hagen.

Well, when the third round of play was over, there was a tremendous surprise. Oh, sure, Vardon and Ray were out in front at 225, but there was another 225 up there on the board and it belonged to Francis Ouimet. Over that rain-drenched course Ouimet had fashioned a 74.

Well, sir, on that final day Ted Ray and Harry Vardon came home in 79 and they were in a tie at 304. But where was Francis Ouimet? Still out on the golf course, that's where he was. When he got to the thirteenth hole, he was in a tough spot. He needed two birdies on the last six holes just to get a tie.

At thirteen, Ouimet chipped in from off the green for one of those two birdies. At fourteen, fifteen and sixteen, he had to settle for pars. Two holes to go and he desperately needed another birdie for the tie. On seventeen he drove well and knocked his second shot up on the green. It was a tough putt that he needed to get the birdie. It was asking too much of a great player, much less an inexperienced twenty-year-old. But Francis knocked the putt in the cup and he had his birdie. Now all he needed was a par four on the last hole and he'd have a tie with Vardon and Ray.

Ouimet drove the ball well, but his second shot was just short of the green. He set himself for the chip. He wanted to get it as close as he could for a gimme putt. But his approach was left five feet away. A really tough putt on any day . . . and on a day like this it must have seemed a dream away. But the dream became a reality, because Ouimet never hesitated. He walked up, took a quick look at the line, and knocked it in. Just like that, he knocked it in. Like you'd do it any old time. He was tied with Vardon and Ray.

The next day, the day of the playoff, it rained. But they played, the two great English pros and the skinny twenty-year-old amateur. And how they played! It was as if destiny were riding on the wrong horse. Not the trained, skilled ones, but the young one, the inexperienced one.

They were all even at the end of nine holes, but on number ten, Ouimet picked up a shot on both Vardon and Ray when they three-putted for fours while he was down in par three. Now the Englishmen started to press. On the fifteenth hole, Ted Ray took a six on a par-four hole. He was now slipping out of contention. But there was still the incomparable Harry Vardon. At seventeen, Vardon too showed the wear and tear by bogeying the hole while Ouimet got a birdie. That was it. It was all over but the shouting. On the last hole Vardon took a double bogey, and although Ray had a birdie, they both had had it. Vardon had finished with 77, Ray with 78, and here was Ouimet running in his final putt for a round of 72. A twenty-year-old American had reserved a page in golf history for himself. From that day on, Francis Ouimet was a golfing immortal.

Walter Hagen, playing his game at Fresh Meadow Country Club in 1939.

What about the other twenty-year-old, Walter Hagen?

If there was one player who made a greater mark on the game of golf than Walter Hagen, you'll have to prove it. No, he wasn't the best of all, but he was right up there with any of them. But even if he hadn't been that great a player, he was still something else, as they say. It was Walter Hagen, more than any other professional, who took the professionals from the back-door entrance and got them to walk in the front door. That's who Walter Hagen was. He could have been a major-league baseball player if he had been so inclined. He was that good an athlete. But he wanted to do it as a golfer. And he did it.

He came out of Rochester, N. Y. He was brash, maybe even cocky. They say that when he got to Brookline in 1913, he walked up to the defending champion, Johnny McDermott, and said, "I've come to help you take care of Vardon and Ray." It was Ouimet who won it, but at the end of 72 holes Hagen was only three shots back and it was a triple bogey at the fourteenth hole that stopped him. It was only a momentary detour. If you will check the record book, you'll see that the winner of the U.S. Open the next year, in 1914, was Walter Hagen. He won the U.S. Open again in 1919. Then he went across the sea and won the British Open four times. Note, too, that he won the P.G.A. championship on five occasions. He won the P.G.A. four times in a row, and it's likely that no one will ever tie that mark.

What of Hagen's great match with Bobby Jones?

In 1926, Hagen was a little upset about the fact that a young amateur named Bobby Jones was being acclaimed as the greatest golfer in the world. In his typical fashion he figured that something like the "greatest golfer in the world" title should be decided on a golf course. He got a friend to arrange a match with Jones. They were to play seventy-two holes. Thirty-six would be played at Bobby Jones's course and thirty-six at Hagen's. It was no contest—the Haig beat Jones twelve and eleven. It was the worst defeat ever suffered by Bobby Jones.

How great was Bobby Jones?

The story has just been told about how Walter Hagen took Bobby Jones apart in their 72-hole match play in 1926. But even champions have their moments of no results. The meeting with Hagen was one of the few contests in which Jones came away empty-handed.

Bobby Jones was destined for greatness from the time he was knee-high to a golf bag. He had it, and everyone who saw him, even when he was a boy, knew it. He had just one problem, and it had nothing to do with hitting the ball or putting the ball. He had a mean temper, a real mean temper, the kind that could keep him from signing a score card as champ. The press got on him about it, and like a balkish colt, he finally was rid of his temper. The rest of the story is history.

When Bobby was fourteen years of age, he led the National Amateur at the end of the first round of the qualifying round. That was in 1916. Four years later, he played a fellow by the name of Francis Ouimet in the semi-

Bobby Jones displaying his long driving style.

finals. He lost, but he was only eighteen. He was to lose quite a few times in those learning years. He even picked up at the British Open in 1922. He was learning.

They played the U.S. Open at the Inwood Country Club in 1923. Robert Tyre Jones, Jr. was now twenty-one years old, one year older than Francis Ouimet was when he had won it in 1913.

The Inwood Country Club is located on Long Island. As long as there is an Inwood Country Club on Long Island, it will be remembered as the course where Bobby Jones won his first U.S. Open. It didn't come easy. It came hard, real hard. Coming to the last round, Jones led the field by three shots. For the last three holes, he merely had to par in to win. He went 5-5-6 on the last three holes whose pars were 4-4-4. When Bobby Cruickshank sank a seven-foot putt on the last hole, it meant a play-off.

They came to the last hole all even, Jones and Cruickshank. Jones had taken a double bogey six the previous day, but with the chips down, Bobby Jones came up with a par while Cruickshank took a double bogey six— and Bobby Jones had won the championship. He was to win the U.S. Open three more times before he quit.

What is Bobby Jones most famous for?

Walter Hagen once said, "If I were asked to vote for the greatest golfer of all time, my vote would go to Bobby Jones." When he said it, he was probably thinking most about what Jones had done in 1930. In that year, Bobby Jones did something no one else had ever done, has ever done since, or probably will ever do. He made the "Grand Slam" of golf. He won the U.S. Amateur, the U.S. Open, the British Amateur and the British Open!

It started with the British Amateur. His toughest match here was against the defending champion, Cyril Tolley, whom he beat one up in nineteen holes. In the final he beat Roger Wethered 7 and 6.

At the British Open he shot 291 to win. He now had two legs on the "Grand Slam."

Back to the United States he came. First it was the Open, played at Interlaken in Minneapolis. He shot 71, 73, 68 and 75 for 287, and the U.S. Open was his.

The Merion Cricket Club was the setting for the National Amateur. It was just a triumphant tour. Jones had no match closer than 5 and 4, and in the final he beat Gene Homans 8 and 7.

That did it for Bobby Jones. He retired then and there at the age of 28. He had won thirteen major championships in eight years. He was known as "Emperor" Jones. He deserved the royal tag.

Gene Sarazan

Which player won the U.S. Open by playing the last 28 holes in 100 strokes?

They call him the Squire. His name is Gene Sarazen, the most durable player the game has known. He trained around 1920, when still a teen-ager, and in the next fifteen years won two U.S. Opens, three P.G.A. championships, the British Open, and the Masters, plus dozens of other tournaments around the world. He tied for the U.S. Open in 1940, losing in a play-off. In his fifties he was still playing sub-par golf.

Now about those 100 shots on the last 28 holes. It took place at Fresh Meadow in 1932. On the final day Gene shot the last ten holes of the morning round in 34. That was like a warm-up, because on the final eighteen holes played in the afternoon he blasted out a 66. It was good enough.

Years later, three to be exact, he sank a 220-yard spoon shot that gave him a double eagle and a tie for the Masters which he won in a play-off with Craig Wood the next day. Sarazen made a specialty out of clutch wins.

How great was Byron Nelson?

There are those who will tell you that no one who ever played the game could hit the ball straighter than Lord Byron. With his picture swing, he'd strike that ball as if he was mechanical.

Nelson played his greatest golf during the early 1940's. He was exempt from service in World War II because he suffered from hemophilia. Actually, Nelson started making his mark on the big-time trail in 1937. That year he won the Masters for the first time. In 1939, the National Open was his in a play-off with Denny Shute and Craig Wood. He won his first P.G.A. in 1940 by beating Sam Snead one up in 36 holes.

Then he won his second Masters in 1942 by outscoring Ben Hogan. But there was more to come. In the two-year period of 1944-45, Nelson was lord and master of all he surveyed. In 1944 Nelson won seven tournaments, and in 1945 he won 19 tournaments, 11 in a row. But his streak was just about over.

In talking about Byron Nelson there has always been a tendency to disparage because many of his wins were scored while some players were away in the service and because his career was rather short. Both of these attitudes are ill-deserved. Nelson did not choose his time, nor did he have control of the illness which hobbled him. In a game where style is a major factor, this man must be rated as one of the greatest stylists of them all.

What about Ben Hogan?

I first saw Hogan play at the Western Open in 1948. To win it, he had to beat Ed "Porky" Oliver in a play-off. Hogan shot 64. He won it. The next year, seemingly on his way to golf's greatest successes, Hogan almost lost his life. It was on February 2, 1949, on one of those lonely Texas highways, that Ben Hogan almost cashed his chips in. He was driving back to his home in Fort Worth on a hazy day when a bus bore down out of nowhere. Instinctively, Hogan flung himself in front of his wife to shield her as the bus and his car collided.

Valerie Hogan, thanks to her husband's heroic action, suffered only minor injuries, but Ben sustained a double fracture of the pelvis, a broken collar bone, a fractured left ankle, and a smashed right rib. He was taken to a hospital in El Paso and apparently was coming out of it all right when he developed a thrombosis (blood clot). In order to stop the clotting, doctors had to tie off the veins in his legs. They saved Hogan's life, but it seemed the end of his golfing career. It might have ended many careers. It didn't end Ben Hogan's.

Ben Hogan blasting out of a wet sand trap.

Sam Snead

What is considered Hogan's greatest feat?

There are those who might point to the fact that he won the U.S. Open four times. So did Bobby Jones and Willie Anderson. I lean toward what he did in 1953 as the highlight of his career. He hadn't been out of the hospital for too long when he won the U.S. Open in 1950. He repeated in 1951. In 1952, Julius Boros interrupted his string. Which brings us to 1953. First, there was the Masters. He shot rounds of 70-69-66-69 for 274. It was a tournament record. In the U.S. Open his total of 283 gave him an easy win—he finished six shots ahead of Sam Snead. Now there was the British Open. He had never been over to play in the British Open, and though his reputation had been established, there was still the matter of the winning of a crown that had graced the heads of great Americans like Hagen, Jones, and Sarazen. Besides which, those Scots had never seen him play. It was like going to the place of origin—so Hogan went. It was cold and rainy all the time. The ball being played, the English ball, was different, smaller, and the conditions on the course were unlike any that Hogan had ever been called upon to face.

But it was the time and the place for the Wee Ice Mon, as the Scots called Hogan. He didn't fail them or their faith in him. It was like a love affair, this feeling of Hogan and the Scots for one another. He proceeded to hammer out 73, 71, 70, and then a 68 for 282 and the British Open. In one year he had won the British and U.S. Opens *and* the Masters!

What great player has never won the U.S. Open?

Even if you're not a big golf fan, you know the answer to this one, because everyone knows Sam Snead. Ask anyone, "Who's the hillbilly from West Virginia who plays golf?" and the answer comes back in torrents. That's how well-known Samuel Jackson Snead is. It really is amazing that this man, who has won well over a hundred tournaments in his life, has never won the Open . . . the U.S. Open, that is. He has won the British Open, and he has won the P.G.A. three times, and he has won the Masters three times, but in all the years he has played he has somehow managed to botch winning the U.S. Open. In his first try in 1937 he finished second to Ralph Guldahl. Everyone who saw him said, "Well, it's just a matter of time." Then, in 1939, he had something happen to him you wouldn't wish on anyone. He came to the last hole needing a five to win and a six to tie. He took an eight. In 1947, he lost in a play-off to Lew Worsham when he missed a little putt after Worsham had asked for a measurement to see who was away. Snead always said that there was no need for the measurement, that everyone could see he was away and should putt first. He was away, and he did putt first, and he missed, and Worsham didn't. Oh, yes, he finished second to Hogan in 1953.

Who is golf's biggest money maker?

The answer can best be supplied by "Arnie's Army." They keep such close tabs on Arnold Palmer that they can tell you the exact amount. If ever a man was born to an age, Arnold Palmer was born for the age of television—the man and the "box" go hand in hand. They were made for one another. No player other than Walter Hagen ever gave the game the "shot" that Arnold Palmer did. Hagen took professional golf from the back door to the front door. Arnold Palmer went from Hagen's Rolls-Royce to the jet airplane. He made the touring pro into a business complex, a complex with many sidelines that went beyond golf. But it all had its beginning with the sport and with the televising of it.

Palmer made his first splash in the National Amateur. It was in 1954 that this bull-strong young man from Latrobe, Pennsylvania, won the title. He then joined the pro ranks. It took a while for the "army" to form, but suddenly all you heard in golf was, "Where's Palmer? How far behind is he?" Arnold Palmer brought the word "charge" into golf. Every Sunday on TV millions would tune in to watch Arnie make his charge. There was the Masters in 1960, for example.

Ken Venturi had come in at 283 and had gone to the clubhouse to try the traditional green jacket on for size—the jacket they give you at Augusta when you win. Out on the course, Arnold Palmer stood at seventeen. He needed a birdie on one of the last two holes for a tie. But seventeen and eighteen at Augusta aren't easy birdie holes. A drive and an eight iron left him 25 feet from the cup on 17. Palmer, with that mobile face, lined up his shot. The stroked putt went to the hole and fell in.

A birdie on 18 now and he would win it. As was the case before, and as it was to remain always, Palmer played 18 with boldness. A tremendous drive, a whistling iron, and he was just five feet from victory. He waved the wand—and there was another birdie in the cup. Ken Venturi had stopped trying coats on for size. In 1960, there was only one size—Arnold Palmer's.

How about the U.S. Open in 1960?

When talk gets around to famous charges that Arnold Palmer has made, you get your choice of quite a few. The one he made down the homestretch at the Cherry Hills course in Denver to win the Open was a classic, though. Going to the last eighteen holes, he was seven shots back of the leader, Big Mike Souchak. But don't get the impression that only Souchak was ahead of Arnie. There were fourteen other fine golfers in front of him, enough of a pack that it seemed only a miracle would do it —give Palmer his first Open win. All right, let's get out the magic wand and wave it. On the first hole, 346 yards, all Palmer did was drive the ball— right over the water and all, he drove it right on the green. Two putts and

a birdie. Then, on the second hole, another birdie; and another on the third; and another on the fourth. On the fifth, Arnie had to settle for a par; but on six and seven, two more birdies. That opening barrage had brought a cluster of six birdies in seven holes. Although he bogied eight, his par on the ninth hole gave him a total of 30 for the first nine holes.

On the back nine he was able to fashion a 35 which, compared to his 30, may not seem magical, but his total of 65 was good enough to win him the U.S. Open.

Arnold Palmer

Who do they call the "Golden Bear"?

That name was tagged on Jack Nicklaus, one of the greatest strikers of the ball the game has ever seen. Nicklaus came out of Columbus, Ohio, as a young boy, much in the fashion of Bobby Jones. While he wasn't able to pull off the "Grand Slam" as an amateur, he spread-eagled the amateur field as no one other than Jones had been able to. At nineteen, he won the first of his two National Amateurs. At twenty, playing in the World Amateur Team championship at the Marion course near Philadelphia, Big Jack shot a 269. That total was 18 better than Hogan had used to win the National Open on the same course in 1950.

Jack Nicklaus putting.

What was special about his winning the U.S. Open?

Jack Nicklaus won the U.S. Open on his first try as a professional. It happened at the Oakmont course in 1962. Jack was all of 22 when he teed off in that competition, and the finish of it was something to see to believe. At the end of seventy-two holes, Nicklaus was in a tie with Arnold Palmer. Palmer at this time was the hottest player in the game. Those who were there and those who watched on television respected the Golden Bear, but against Arnold Palmer . . . forget it. No one was going to beat Arnie in the clutch. Nicklaus did, though. He beat Arnold Palmer that day—and then, a few weeks later when they met head-to-head in a 36-hole test for the televised World Series, Nicklaus did it again. As it turned out, Nicklaus was to be the chink in Arnie's armor, the fly in his ointment. Suddenly, where there had been one man with his feet on top of the golfing world, there were now two men astride and the younger one was pushing the other off, that younger one being Nicklaus.

Why hasn't Nicklaus won the crowds over?

It could be that people were so caught up with Arnold Palmer that they didn't need anyone else. Not only didn't need anyone else, but maybe even didn't like anyone else threatening Arnie's position. Palmer was like apple pie—a legend and an American folk hero. More than that, though, there just was no glamour about Nicklaus. Matter of fact, when you get down to cases, Jack Nicklaus is bland. In golf, there's no such thing as the bland leading the bland. This is not to take anything away from the Golden Bear. The facts are pretty plain for all to see. He's won everything in sight—the Amateur, the U.S. and British Opens, the Masters, the P.G.A.—so he has no glamour to go with his gold. He just happened to come along when the greatest glamour figure, Arnold Palmer, was around. There are other great players over whom Palmer cast a giant shadow, too.

Who are some of these players?

Let's start with a fellow named Billy Casper. Like Nicklaus, all Casper can do is win. About the only thing anyone ever mentions about Billy Casper when they're not talking about his great game is the matter of his exotic diet. Casper, when he first came on the golfing scene, was what you would call a chubby type. You might even have called him fat. He went on a diet which included wild buffalo meat and other uncommon foods. But after you've talked about his diet, what else is new? Well, let's see what else is new. Casper beat Palmer head-to-head in a play-off for the U.S. Open in 1966. He had won it once before in 1959. And along with Palmer and Nicklaus he has one of those special places in the United States mint where they make money. Casper is one of the biggest money-earners of all time. Then you can add the name of Gary Player to the list. This strong little man from South Africa is truly one of the finest players of the game.

What players have won professional golf's Grand Slam?

The Grand Slam in professional golf consists of the U.S. Open, the British Open, the Masters, and the P.G.A. There are only four men who've turned this trick—Ben Hogan, Gene Sarazen, Jack Nicklaus and Gary Player. No one has ever been able to do it in the same year.

What is the longest hole in one ever made?

Would you believe 444 yards? Robert Mitera of Omaha, Nebraska, knocked his tee shot into the cup on the tenth hole at the Miracle Hills Golf Club in Omaha. It took place on October 7, 1965, and it broke the old record which had been held by a former baseball player named Lou Kretlow. That mark had been a mere 427 yards. Incidentally, the odds of making a hole in one are listed at more than a million to one, so if you've never gotten a hole in one, don't feel bad.

Mickey Wright, voted Woman Athlete of the Year for 1964.

"Babe" Didrikson Zaharias

What about the lady golfers?

There have been some really great women golfers. As a matter of fact, there are some great ones around right now. One of the gals, Mickey Wright, is considered by some experts as having the best "swing" in the business. In 1963, she won thirteen of the twenty-eight tournaments she entered. Mickey is a big gal at 5′8½″ and 140 pounds, and when she hits the ball it doesn't know that it's a woman who pounded it. The golf ball is no respecter of sex, only of power, and Mickey Wright has plenty of that. So does the big gal from Texas, Kathy Whitworth. She can knock the ball out there as far as most men. And there's another lady golfer, this one an amateur who answers to the name of Jo Anne Gunderson Carner.

Who was golf's best known lady player?

There can be plenty of debate about "the best player," but there's no doubt that more people knew "Babe" Didrikson Zaharias than any other player. Mildred Didrikson Zaharias came out of Texas, and in a state that prides itself on the fact that their athletes are special, the Babe was extra-special. She first came to the attention of sports fans in the 1932 Olympics, winning the woman's 80-meter hurdles and javelin throw. She also tied for first in the high jump, but was disqualified for diving over the bar. It was a mere technicality, because it was later legalized. So the "Babe" had to settle for "just" two gold medals.

The "Babe" then took up the game of golf. She and the game were made for one another. For sheer power, there probably were few that could match her. But, as the saying goes, "you drive for show and putt for dough." So the "Babe" learned how to play. It was only a matter of time before she won the National Amateur. A little more time and she added the British Amateur title to her list.

Then when she turned pro, she had to beat some of the best to win the Women's Open. There were fine players like Patty Berg, Louise Suggs, the Bauer sisters, Beverly Hanson, Betty Jameson, and Betsy Rawls. The "Babe" won the Women's Open three times before she succumbed to cancer on September 27, 1956. It's no overstatement to say that she was as great an athlete as sports has ever seen.

Who was Joyce Wethered?

When you ask old-timers about the player who had the best swing ever in golf, you expect to hear, "Well, it could be Harry Vardon, or Sam Snead, or Byron Nelson." You'd be surprised to know, though, that many oldsters would pick the great English lady golfer, Joyce Wethered, over any male player. Miss Wethered did not play for too long, but in the short span of time she did, her swing was so great that many male players tried to copy it. No one ever did. There was only one Joyce Wethered.

Wichita's Jim Ryun beating Peter Snell of New Zealand in a mile run.

Track and Field

To speculate on how track and field events began is something like asking how man learned to do business. "As soon as the urge struck him," might apply. Did Adam suggest to Eve that he could outrun her to the apple? Or did running begin when some man of some ancient era chose not to tangle with some animal and decided to outrun it? If he got tired, he probably picked up a rock and threw it at the creature in pursuit, So we have running and throwing and hurdling and jumping and all of the other things that came naturally. The Greeks, of course, began what may be the oldest of sports competition, the Olympics. They were held regularly until A.D. 392 when they were banned by a Roman emperor. At that time they had had a run of some eleven centuries. In 1892, a young French Baron, Pierre de Coubertin, proposed renewing the Olympics at a meeting of the Athletic Sports Union in Paris. No one took it too seriously, but in 1894, at an athletic congress, de Coubertin enlisted more support, and *voila!* the Olympics came into being again in 1896.

Bob Beamon digs his feet into the sand after a record-shattering long jump.

What is considered the greatest Olympic feat?

Most experts now feel that when Bob Beamon went into orbit in the long jump and didn't come down till 29′2½″ later, man had made his most awesome feat. The previous world's record in the long jump, set at 26′8¼″ by Jesse Owens on May 25, 1935, had stood for twenty-five years! That should give you an idea of what it was like to break a record in this particular event. It wasn't tough—it was well nigh impossible. Then, when it was finally broken by Ralph Boston in 1960, the mark went to 26′11¼″. Finally, Ralph Boston and the great Russian, Igor Ter-Ovanesyan, broke the 27-foot barrier. The impossible had been accomplished. Could anyone dare dream that 28 feet might some day be leaped? It may seem overdramatic, but when Beamon exploded off the mark at Mexico City and not only went better than 28 feet but better than 29 feet, it was as if time had leaped forward with him. A stupendous and memorable accomplishment!

What other memorable moments occurred in the 1968 Olympics?

Where do you begin in relating what happened at Mexico City? O.K., start with the short events. Jim Hines ran a 9.9-second hundred meter (a new world's record). Tommie Smith set a new world's record in the 200-

meter run with a clocking of 19.8. In the 400 meter, Lee Evans ran an incredible 43.8 to break the 44-second barrier. There were other winners who didn't set world records, like Kipchoge Keino in the 1500-meter run, but his time of 3.34.9 at that altitude was an outstanding accomplishment. Mention should be made of Dave Hemery's world record in the 400-meter hurdles. The time of 48.1 was needed to beat the tough field he ran against. There is a feeling that the most overlooked win in the Olympics was in the Triple Jump where the Russian, Viktor Saneyev, leaped 57'¾". No one had ever been over 56 feet before competition began that day at Mexico City, and while Saneyev wasn't the first over 56 feet, he was the first ever over 57 feet.

Who turned in the greatest one-day performance in track history?

It is generally conceded that Jesse Owens turned the trick at the Big Ten Championships in Ann Arbor, Michigan, on May 25, 1935, when he set four world records in one day. Jesse ran the 220-yard dash in 20.3 seconds, breaking the world record by 0.3; he knocked 0.4 off the 220-yard low-hurdles record with a 22.6 clocking; he broke the broad-jump record by 6⅛ inches with a leap of 26–8¼; and he tied the 100-yard-dash record of 9.4!

In 1936, Jesse set a new world record for 100 meters (10.2) and ran on the American team that set a world record of 39.8 for the 400-meter relay in the Olympic finals. Only three men

U.S. sprint star Jesse Owens at the 1936 Olympics.

Bob Hayes

ever defeated Jesse Owens in a sprint race—Ralph Metcalfe, Eulace Peacock, and James Johnson.

In a world-wide poll of sports experts, Jesse Owens was voted "Athlete of the Half-Century" for the years 1900–1950. He ended his career by turning professional to run on foot against race horses, which gives you a good idea of the professional possibilities open to track stars.

Another great Negro sprinter, Bob Hayes, ended his career by signing a professional football contract. In 60 races at 100 yards and 100 meters, including five 9.1 clockings at 100 yards, Hayes lost only twice.

Who were the only two men ever to beat Bob Hayes?

They were Harry Jerome, Canada's greatest sprinter, and Roger Sayers, whose brother Gale joined Hayes as a National Football League rookie sensation in 1965. Incidentally, after losing to Jerome and Sayers in the same week in 1962, Hayes ran up a string of 44 straight victories (including the Olympic 100 meters) before turning pro.

Another Olympic 100-meters champion had a streak almost twice as long as Hayes'—but not in the sprints. This great hurdler, whose boyhood idol was Jesse Owens, won 82 consecutive races, indoors and out, a feat doubly remarkable because of the ever-present danger of hitting a hurdle and losing stride; there aren't many winning streaks in the hurdles.

What great hurdler was also an Olympic 100-meter champion?

His name was Harrison Dillard, and he ran the Olympic sprint instead of the hurdles because in the USA's 1948 Olympic trials he hit several hurdles and could not finish the race. Dillard showed he was a real champion by coming back to make the team in the 100 meters, and then winning at the London Olympics. Four years later, "Bones" came out of retirement to win the Olympic high-hurdles title at Helsinki.

Because the high hurdles are 3 feet, 6 inches high, tall hurdlers have an advantage over short ones, 5'10" being considered the minimum height for a good hurdler. Yet one 5'10" hurdler was as good as they come, winning nine National AAU high-hurdles championships, and carving out his own unbeaten streak of 55 victories in indoor races from 1960 through 1964.

Who was the short high hurdler who won the 1964 Olympic gold medal in his event?

Hayes Jones. Jones, who used great speed and perfect hurdling form to overcome his lack of height, really "owned" the indoor hurdles. In fact, when he retired he held the meet record in his event in every one of the 18 major indoor meets. Although he never held the outdoor world record, Jones went on to win the 1964 Olympic gold medal in the high hurdles.

You might think that the female Jesse Owens would be Wilma Rudolph, but you'd be wrong. At one time, in 1948, a Dutch housewife held seven world records at once, including the 100 yards, 100 meters, high jump, broad jump and 80-meters hurdles.

How many Kansans have held world records in the middle distances?

Glenn Cunningham, Archie San Romani, Wes Santee and, of course, Jim Ryun. But at the time this book was written, only Cunningham and

Ryun ever held the mile record. San Romani's record was for 2,000 meters and Santee's for 1,500 meters (the "Metric Mile"). Ryun also holds the record at 880 yards. Cunningham set his mile record, 4:06.8, in 1934. He actually ran a 4:04.4 mile indoors, but it was paced by a quartet of quarter-milers and was never accepted as a record.

Glenn Cunningham

Who has run more under-four-minutes miles than anyone else?

Peter Snell of New Zealand broke four minutes 15 times, but Herb Elliott of Australia did it *17* times! Even more remarkable, Elliott, although he scorned weak opposition and constantly raced against the best runners in the world, never lost a mile or 1,500 meters race.

Many track fans feel that a strong finishing kick is the secret of success in the mile. "Give me a miler who can sprint," they say, "and he'll come from behind to win in the homestretch.

How important is a big "kick" to a miler?

Not nearly as important as most people think. Cordner Nelson, editor of *Track & Field News,* recently analyzed 89 important mile and 1,500 meter races to find out. He discovered that the leader coming into the homestretch won 82 per cent of those races. Running is just like every other human activity . . . you can't afford to leave everything till the last minute.

Peter Snell

How many men have held seven or more world records at one time?

Four: Paavo Nurmi of Finland, Gunder Hagg of Sweden, Emil Zatopek of Czechoslovakia, and Ron Clarke of Australia—all distance runners. Nurmi set his records from 1922 through 1931, Hagg ruled the roost in the Forties until he was declared a professional in 1945, Zatopek, a Czech army officer, was supreme in the Fifties, and Clarke is still running today.

Which four American runners have held world records at two miles or over?

Most sports fans know that Bob Schul held the two-mile record in 1964-65, and that Billy Mills and Gerry Lindgren ran a near dead-heat as both set a new six-mile record in 1965. The hard one is Don Lash, the great Indiana distance man of the middle 1930's. Lash, running in the Princeton Invitational in 1936, became the first American ever to hold a world record at a distance longer than a mile, breaking Nurmi's mark of 8:59.6 with an 8:58.4 performance. Three and a half months later, Hockert, another Finn, took Lash's record away from him by running 8:57.4.

Long before the fiberglass pole made 16- and 17-foot pole vaults commonplace, Cornelius Warmerdam startled the world with the first 15-foot

Don Lash taking the lead and winning race.

Cornelius Warmerdam clearing the bar.

clearance. In fact, between 1940 and 1944, "Dutch" Warmerdam bettered 15 feet outdoors 43 times! It wasn't until seven years later that anyone else vaulted 15 feet outdoors. Then two men did it on the same day!

Which two pole vaulters cleared 15 feet on the same day?

Don Cooper of Nebraska and Don Laz of Illinois became history's second and third 15-footers on April 21, 1951. Bob Richards, the "Vaulting Vicar" who had already cleared the height in indoor meets that winter, didn't join Cooper and Laz with an outdoor clearance until three weeks later, on May 11.

Warmerdam used a bamboo pole; Richards and Don Bragg used a steel pole; and although fiberglass poles were being used as early as 1952 (by decathlon man Bob Mathias), the "glass" pole didn't become popular until lesser-known vaulters catapulted to 16-foot vaults using it. John Uelses made the first 16-foot vault in 1962, and John Pennel first cleared 17 feet a year later.

How much extra height does the fiberglass pole provide?

Experts estimate that the fiberglass pole can add nearly two feet to a vaulter's efforts, but they hasten to add that the gymnastics involved in mastering fiberglass-pole technique are far more difficult than vaulting with a bamboo or a metal pole.

Some athletes prefer to do their jumping without a pole, but not all of them disdain using equipment that might help them a bit.

After Charley Dumas set a world record by high-jumping 7 feet, ½ inch, John Thomas and Valery Brumel later raised the mark to almost unbelievable heights. But between Dumas and Thomas, another Russian, Yuri Stepanov, became the first non-American in history to hold the high-jump record. A storm of controversy raged around his record.

High-jumper John Thomas.

Why was Yuri Stepanov's high-jump record called into question?

When Yuri Stepanov bettered Dumas' record with a 7'1" jump in Moscow in 1957, he wore a special shoe with a built-up sole approximately an inch thick. The German press dubbed it the "Catapult-shoe," and the International Amateur Athletic Federation withheld recognition of the record for more than a year while debating if use of the shoe was unfair. Finally, the IAAF accepted the record as valid, and then immediately contradicted itself by banning the shoe.

Thomas and Brumel staged a series of epic stratospheric battles, with the Russian winning all but one of them. But their friendly two-man feud ended when Brumel retired after being injured in a Moscow scooter accident.

What were John Thomas' and Valery Brumel's highest jumps?

Thomas' best was 7'3¾", a world record when he cleared it at the 1960 Olympic trials. Brumel improved the record to 7'4", then 7'4½" in 1961, cleared 7'5" and 7'5½" in 1962, and finally reached 7'5¾" at the 1963 USA-Russia meet at Moscow in 1963.

Another classic two-man rivalry between an American and a Russian has been staged in the broad jump between Ralph Boston and Igor Ter-Ovanesyan. Ralph and "Ter" have become good friends over the years, but Igor has never won from Boston outdoors.

Valery Brumel of the Soviet Union.

In what year did Parry O'Brien retire from the shot put?

Most world records are the result of keen competition. But Parry O'Brien was so much better than his fellow shot-putters that over the years 1952-58 he lost only three times in nearly 200 meets. Yet Parry broke the world record in the shot *16* times, improving it from 58′10½″ to 63′4″ in seven years. In May, 1966, the durable Parry won 14 indoor and outdoor national championships in the shot-put, and developed a new style of putting which revolutionized the event.

In 1965, Randy Matson became the new king of the shot-put with a heave of 70′7¼″ while he was a sophomore at Texas A&M. Between O'Brien and Matson, though, a couple of pretty fair shot-putters held the coveted world record.

Parry O'Brien puts the shot.

Who held the shot-put record between 1960 and 1965?

Bill Neider broke O'Brien's record in 1960 with a mark of 65′10″, and Dallas Long eventually raised the record to 67′10″ in 1964 before Matson took over. Neider was the 1960 Olympic champion at Rome, and Long won the Olympic title at Tokyo in 1964.

In the first USA-USSR meet, Rafer Johnson took the world-decathlon record away from Vasily Kuznetsov of the Soviets. Although Kuznetsov regained the record in May, 1960, Johnson recaptured it in July and went on to win the Olympic decathlon in September from C. K. Yang and Kuznetsov. Johnson was almost unbeatable, but he did lose once.

What are the ten events of the decathlon?

The word "decathlon" comes from the Greek words *deca,* ten, and *athlon,* a contest. In modern track and field, it consists of ten events, contested over a two-day program.

First day: 100-meter dash, broad jump, shot-put, high jump, 440-yard run. Second day: 110-meter high hurdles, discus throw, pole vault, javelin throw, and 1,500-meter run.

Who was the only man to defeat Rafer Johnson?

Milt Campbell of Plainfield, New Jersey, and Indiana University was the only man to defeat Rafer Johnson in a decathlon. Big Milt scored when it counted, too, winning the gold medal at Melbourne in the 1956 Olympics. Johnson was second, with Kuznetsov, as usual, close behind.

One woman in track history was as versatile as Rafer Johnson. In the 1932 Women's AAU meet, this Texas girl, competing as a one-woman team, won five national championships plus the team title. At one time or another, she set world records in the hurdles, the high jump and the javelin, and later became the greatest woman golfer of her time.

Mildred ("Babe") Didrikson (far right) winning the first heat of the 80-meter hurdles when she first appeared on the sporting scene.

Who was America's greatest woman athlete?

She was Mildred "Babe" Didrikson. On that memorable day in 1932 the 18-year-old Babe scored 30 points all by herself, while the runner-up team of more than 20 women from the Illinois AC scored only 22 points. Besides winning five events outright, Babe also tied for first in the high jump —with a new world record of 5'3–3/16"!

Who was the woman track star who held seven world records at once?

She was Francina ("Fanny") Blankers-Koen, and although she was 30 years old in 1948, she went on to produce *two more* world records. At age 32, Fanny set a new standard for the 220-yard dash, and at 33 she proved she was still the world's most versatile trackswoman by setting a new world record in the pentathlon, raising the mark by an amazing 771 points to 4,692 points. That's like knocking 20 seconds off a mile record!

Of all running events, the mile seems to be the most fascinating to the fans. And Kansas seems to be the place where great milers grow best in the United States. Four Kansas milers have become world record holders.

Tennis

Helen Wills Moody

The game of tennis as we know it today was invented in 1873 by a Major Walter Clopton Wingfield in Wales in the British Isles. It was adapted from the game of court tennis, a game which historians trace back to the thirteenth century. Actually, as in the case of almost every sport, you'll find some who will find origins of a game where no origins seem possible. In the case of court tennis, there have been some theories advanced about the game having been played in Egypt.

At any rate, we know that Major Wingfield invented the game we call lawn tennis in 1873.

When was the game introduced in the United States?

The exact date has never been firmly set. A court was built by Hollis Hunnewell and Nathaniel Thayer on Buckingham Street, Boston, on the site that is now Back Bay Station. The year was 1876. This is really the most tangible evidence regarding the first playing of the game in the United States, although there are suspicions that the game was played earlier.

A terrific tennis trio: (left) Bill Tilden; (center) Don Budge, about to use the finest backhand in the history of tennis; and (right) Don Laver, the sensational Australian, returning a shot.

Who is considered the greatest player of all time?

Each era has its great one and people of that era like to think their champion is the best. So it is in tennis. When it gets down to cases, there's usually a group that says, "Tilden was the best," or "Budge was the greatest," or "Jack Kramer," or "Pancho Gonzales," or "Ellsworth Vines." Then, among the moderns, you'll hear votes for some of the Australians like Rod Laver.

If you go for both ability and longevity, it's pretty hard to keep from picking Bill Tilden. It's not only how well he played, but how long. He beat the best over quite a period of time and he was the complete virtuoso. He ranked number one in the amateurs from 1919 through 1929. Then he turned pro and dominated the play-for-pay boys till he was toppled by Ellsworth Vines. He did it all—serve, volley, ground strokes, tactics and court coverage. He'd play you any way you wanted, from base-line to net. He was colorful, controversial and complete.

142

How many players have won Tennis' Grand Slam?

The Grand Slam in tennis consists of winning the Australian, British, French and United States championships. It has been accomplished only twice. Don Budge of the United States turned the trick in 1938 and Rod Laver of Australia did it in 1962. At the beginning of his career, around 1933, Don Budge became convinced that to do well in the big time, he would have to do something about his forehand—his backhand was one of the most lethal in the history of the game. Accordingly, in the bulldog fashion typical of all greats, he went back home to California and spent a year with a coach working on the stroke. The rest is history. Laver was a link in the chain of superstars developed by Harry Hopman, the famous Australian coach, that included Ken Rosewall, Lew Hoad, Frank Sedgman, and Neale Fraser. Laver was taken out of school at sixteen to concentrate on tennis and developed such a powerful game that when he turned pro, it did not take him long to dominate the field.

When did open tennis begin?

In a historic reversal of policy, the International Lawn Tennis Federation officially approved open tennis at a meeting in Paris on March 30, 1968. Credit for the policy shift was attributed to Britain and its liberal tennis association which had voted to open its own major tournaments to amateurs and pros with or without international approval. The reaction to open tennis was even greater than had been expected. The first open was held in Bournemouth, England, in April. Two Australian professionals— Ken Rosewall and Rod Laver—met in the finals with Rosewall winning 3-6, 6-2, 6-0, 6-3. Laver, considered the world's greatest player, then won the first Wimbledon Open Title by defeating Tony Roche in straight sets. For Laver, it was his third Wimbledon crown. He had won previously as an amateur in 1961 and 1962. Only one other man has ever won three Wimbledon singles championships. Fred Perry, the great British player, turned the trick as an amateur in 1934, 1935, and 1936.

How did the Davis Cup originate?

The late Dwight Davis, then a 21-year-old senior at Harvard and an enthusiast of the game, spent $800 in 1900 for the trophy that has assumed his name. He intended the cup for an international competition, to be kept by victorious nations. Under the rules, the nation that wins the cup holds it for a year, then meets the nation that survives an elimination tournament in what is called the challenge round. (Luckily, you can't copyright titles.) In cup play, there are four singles matches and a doubles match. To win, a nation must take three of the five matches.

Which nation has won the Davis Cup most times?

At the end of Davis Cup competition in 1968, Australia with 22 wins was the leader. The United States has won the cup twenty times, Britain nine times, and France six times. Since World War II, Australia has won the cup fifteen times and the United States eight. Australian dominance has been so great that since 1950 they have won it fifteen of nineteen tries. In 1968, the United States claimed the cup for the first time in five years. In winning it, the Americans depended on their great singles players, Arthur Ashe and Clark Graebner, and their doubles team of Stan Smith and Robert Lutz. Should Davis Cup play become open, it might provide an even further Australian domination.

Who was considered the most successful Davis Cup coach in history?

Harry Hopman of Australia. His formula: intensive physical training and emphasis on the theory of "hitting for the lines." Hopman's abrasive personality has made him many enemies, particularly among the press, but his pupils swear by him. Among the many stars he has developed in his time are Frank Sedgman, Ken McGregor, Lew Hoad, Ken Rosewall, Neale Fraser, and Rod Laver.

Arthur Ashe

Frank Sedgman

Helen Jacobs

Who won the first American Open?

This honor fell to the great American amateur, Arthur Ashe. In the face of as strong an open field as could be put together, Ashe, a lieutenant in the armed forces of the United States, defeated Tom Okker of the Netherlands in a fiercely fought final, 14-12, 5-7, 6-3, 3-6, 6-3. As an amateur, Ashe was ineligible for prize money. Okker, a 24-year-old amateur who registered for prize money in conjunction with international rules, won the $14,000 top prize. Ashe collected $280 in expense money.

Who was the most dominant figure in U.S. women's tennis?

Helen Wills, who ranked first seven times and won the singles title seven times, the last time in 1931. Two years later, in 1933, she made a comeback and reached the final with Helen Jacobs. With the score 8-6, 3-6, 3-0 against her, she paused dramatically on the court, walked to the umpire's chair and said with her characteristic poker face: "Please tell my opponent I am unable to continue because of a strained back." There was no love lost between the two stars, and Miss Jacobs, who had won the title the previous year, was to go on to take it a total of four times.

What was the golden era of tennis?

From 1920 to 1930, the sports pages were filled with the names of Bill Tilden, Billy Johnston, Vinnie Richards and R. Norris Williams. The ballyhoo over their matches across the country created thousands of fans. In 1926, a match was played that put tennis on the front pages; it was between Suzanne Lenglen of France, called the greatest woman player in the world, and Helen Wills, the all-American girl—calm, cool and efficient. Suzanne won, 6-3, 8-6, although Helen nearly evened matters in the second set. But it gave tennis a tremendous impetus. The loser became "Our Helen" and "Queen Helen," the biggest drawing card in the game except for Tilden. The four musketeers from France then appeared on the scene and began to close in on America's best. Rene Lacoste beat Tilden in 1926 and led his compatriots to victory the following year by beating Tilden and Johnson. The three other musketeers were Henri Cochet, Jean Borotra and Jacques Brugnon. These four dominated the sport for the next six years.

Why are some players better on a grass court and others better on a clay court?

The difference is in the bounce and spin as the ball strikes the surface. A big server has the advantage on grass because his ball skids as it hits, forcing a weak return that he should be able to put away. On clay, his serve is not nearly so effective because the ball will "come up" after striking the surface. On grass, it is dangerous to stay on the base-line because of the peril of bad bounces, so the idea is to get the commanding position at the net as soon as possible. On clay, the movement of the ball is slower, thus making it easier to retrieve shots. Steadiness and patience are required to win a clay match—that is, being able to keep the ball in play from the backcourt and waiting for the right approach to the net. The volleyer is more vulnerable to the passing shot on clay, as the ball will "hang" and allow his opponent time to put it by him.

What was the biggest crowd ever to see a Davis Cup tennis match?

About 26,000 people turned out at Kooyong Stadium in Melbourne, Australia, in 1953, when Australia defeated the United States, 3-2, in the challenge round. Wimbledon, site of the British championship, has drawn up to thirty thousand in a day of play. The Forest Hills Stadium in Queens, scene of the United States nationals, has a capacity of 14,500, which has often been exceeded.

Are there any small tennis players who have become great champions?

Yes, Bryan ("Bitsy") Grant of Atlanta, who was in the top ten from 1933 to 1941, except 1940. Grant was five feet six inches tall and stayed on top of the game through his remarkable retrieving ability. His steadiness discouraged his opponents; they could not get the ball past him. He was a master at strategy and in the use of spin and drop shots; he was also a superb doubles player. Another is Ken Rosewall (five-eight), the master of control and possessor of what is generally considered the best backhand in the game. An artist in both the backcourt and forecourt, quick and clever, he took over the professional championship from Pancho Gonzalez. Now coming up is Joaquin LayoMayo of Mexico, who's five-six.

Bryon ("Bitsy") Grant dives to get a fast one.

What has been the major change in tennis since the days of Tilden and Budge?

There was more base-line play in those days. Today, a player goes to the net regularly behind his serve and tries to put the ball away with his volley for the point. This serve-volley pattern has been copied so avidly that many fans feel it is producing boring tennis. Yet it is skillful, winning tennis, and, as I said before, as long as it pays off in victories and the rules are not altered, it will continue to be practiced by major players.

What is the Wightman Cup?

It is a trophy donated by the "all-time great," Hazel Hotchkiss Wightman, for a women's competition between England and the United States. The series began in 1923 and is played annually. Three women on each team play a total of five singles matches and there are two doubles matches, making a total of seven matches. Over the years England has won six times and the U.S. thirty-one.

In tennis, as in other sports, the big man has the advantage. But there have been some notable exceptions.

How many great players have two-handed shots?

The best today is Cliff Drysdale of South Africa, who has remarkable control of his two-handed backhand and uses it to score heavily. Mike Belkin of Miami Beach, ranked seventh in the United States, also hits his backhand with the two-fisted grip. Pancho Segura of Ecuador whaled the ball with two hands from both forehand and backhand, and was so good that he was able to earn a world ranking in the early 1940's. Billy Lenoir of Arizona and Jim McManus of California are others with two-fisted backhands. In the 1930's, Vivian McGrath and Jack Bromwich of Australia were the greatest exponents of that style. Bromwich, especially, was a master in doubles, as he had a talent for disguising his shots.

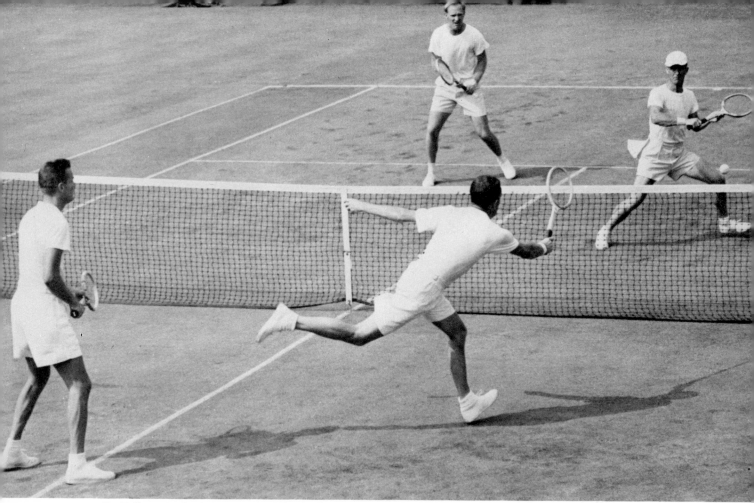

Billy Talbert (right forecourt) hits the ball in a Davis Cup Doubles battle. His partner at left is Gardner Mulloy.

Who was the player who rose to fame despite having diabetes?

Billy Talbert. Helped by insulin injection and pills and special exercises, this Cincinnati-born start played for many years in top competition, gaining high rank. Talbert had to modify his game to cope with his ailment. He knew that he would weaken in long matches, so he developed an effort-saving style. For instance, he was famous for his short-swing serve and the economy of his ground strokes. The highest ranking he achieved was third in 1949. He was unsurpassed as a doubles player, winning the national crown with Gar Mulloy four times. He went on to captain the Davis Cup team, although he fell in disfavor with the bigwigs because of his independence. Today he is regarded as the elder statesman of tennis because of his experience and his thorough knowledge of the game.

What is VASSS?

Many people, especially the uninitiated, are dismayed over the complexity of the scoring system in tennis—all those aces, deuces, ads, and loves. But something is now being done about it.

It is the Van Alen Simplified Scoring System, devised by James Van Alen of Newport, Rhode Island, president of the Tennis Hall of Fame. The system is based primarily on the table tennis idea of scoring, and therefore there are no deuces and ads. A match consists of 31 points. The chief aim of VASSS is to shorten matches. The pros have adopted the system in the belief that it produces more exciting tennis for spectators. There have been only a few amateur VASSS tournaments, because U.S. Lawn Tennis Association officials have shown a cool attitude toward the system. Van Alen has been plugging it for six years and is determined to put it across for what he calls the betterment of the game.

Why has Australia become such a dominant tennis nation?

Australia has a tremendous number of tennis courts in ratio to its population. Tennis is the country's national game and is played day and night. Promising young players are taken in hand by coaches and officials, and given every opportunity to improve. This is part of an all-encompassing junior program that is the envy of other nations. When Margaret Smith, the great Australian lady player, started to learn the game, she had only to step outside her house to have a choice of forty grass courts on which to practice. When astronauts flew over Australia at night, the lights from the tennis courts caught their attention. Good coaching has also played an important role in the development of Aussie stars. Harry Hopman, the Davis Cup captain, is recognized all over the world as one of the best coaches in the game. All of these factors go into the making of great Australian players.

Jack Kramer

Do top singles players make good doubles players?

Not necessarily. The reason is that doubles play requires more varied types of shots. In addition, it also calls for teamwork and special strategy. For success in doubles, the two players must learn to blend their talents so that they may present the strongest front while attacking and defending. Each must be ready to sacrifice himself for the good of the team. The serve, volley, and overhead are the three most important weapons in doubles, and usually the team that is "hitting down," not "up," comes out on top.

Among the great doubles teams have been the aforementioned Talbert and Mulloy; Don Budge and Gene Mako; George Lott and Johnny Doeg (Lott won the U.S. doubles title a record total of five times, twice with Les Stoefen, twice with Johnny Doeg, and once with John Hennessey); Bill Tilden and Vinnie Richards (although Tilden was said to have disliked doubles play); Jack Kramer and Ted Schroeder; John Bromwich and Frank Sedgman of Australia; Neale Fraser and Roy Emerson of Australia; and Ken Rosewall and Lew Hoad of Australia.

Tennis siblings: (left) Nancy Richey and (right) Cliff Richey.

What is the outstanding brother-sister act in tennis today?

The Richeys of San Angelo, Texas. Cliff is one of the finest men players in the United States. Sister Nancy is equally outstanding among the lady players. Cliff was taken out of high school by his father, who has coached him and sent out on the world tour. Nancy, who at one time was co-ranked number one with the great Mrs. Billie Jean King, is three years older than Cliff and a mighty fine competitor. The two are sharply different personalities. Cliff has been involved in many tempestuous outbreaks on the court, but Nancy is placid. They never play doubles together because, as each has said, "it just doesn't work."

What is the Federation Cup?

It is the women's version of the Davis Cup, originating in 1963. The United States has won it twice and Australia has won it twice. In 1966, the matches were held in Turin, Italy, with sixteen nations competing. The U.S. teams consisted of Mrs. King, Julie Heldman, and Carole Graebner. The American girls defeated Germany in the finals. Australia had been favored, but suffered a setback when top star Margaret Smith was injured and unable to play. The matches consist of two singles and one doubles.

Who is rated the greatest woman player?

As with the men's section, the debate about the greatest lady player is one that could go on all night. But there is a tendency to lean to the great French player, Suzanne Lenglen. Lenglen was a fiery competitor and a fine all-around player. Miss Lenglen, as was pointed out earlier, beat the woman who is considered by some to be the greatest, Helen Wills Moody, when they met head to head. It could be argued, though, that Mrs. Moody had not yet reached her greatest peak when she played the French star. It could also be pointed out that Mrs. Moody won at Wimbledon and in France, as well as the United States. Strangely, Lenglen never won the American championship.

Suzanne Lenglen

Who are some of the other great men players?

It would simply be impossible to talk tennis and leave out some mention of great players like Pancho Gonzales, Jack Kramer, and Ellsworth Vines. Let's talk first about Kramer, who served the game both as player and promoter. As a player, he had few peers and virtually no superiors. He did not have an amateur record to match either Bill Tilden or Don Budge, but he did win at both Forest Hills and at Wimbledon, and was key man on the successful Davis Cup team. When he turned pro, he came into his own. From 1948 to 1953 he beat them all on the professional tour. Then, feeling that he had no more worlds to conquer, Kramer turned all of his talent to promoting world tours.

His successor was Richard "Pancho" Gonzales, who, after having won the American amateur title, decided to take on Kramer in 1949. Gonzales was not up to the task and went down to defeat. But he hit the comeback trail in 1951, and by 1954 he was the king of the tour. I mentioned earlier that Bill Tilden had played for many years. About the only man who can rival Tilden for longevity is Gonzales. The incredible Californian was still playing in 1969 and giving almost as well as he took.

There may be some to whom the name of Ellsworth Vines will be meaningless. That's too bad, for when he burst upon the tennis scene, he was a meteor. He hit the ball like it was going out of style. There probably has never been a player who hit the ball harder. From 1934 to 1939, playing professionally, Vines won 257 times and lost 130 matches against the best. The only player to win a majority of matches against him was another great Californian, Don Budge. Against Tilden, Vines won 61 and lost 19, and though the old master, Tilden, was beyond his prime, it was still a considerable feat to beat him at any time.

These were the greats in a sport that has seen many who trod the turf with giant strides.

Pancho Gonzales

Ellsworth Vines

155

INDEX

(Numerals in *italics*
refer to pictures

A

Aaron, Henry, 14
Adams, Babe, 24
Adcock, Joe, 12, 19
Akron Professionals, 51
Alabama, University of,
46, 49
Alcindor, Lew, 56, *57,*
58, 68
Alexander, Grover
Cleveland, 17, 19, 20
Ali, Muhammed, 78, *80,*
81, 88
All-Americans, 41, 43, 58
all-court press, 69
All-Star Game, 28-30
Amateur Hockey
Association, 103
Ameche, Alan, 48, 49
American Association, 15
American Baseball
League, 9, 15, 17, 20,
23, 28, 29, 30
American Basketball
League, 66
American Football
League, 31, 48, 52
American Legion League,
6
American Professional
Football Association, 51
Anderson, Willie, 105,
108, 118
Anson, Adrian ("Cap"),
14
Armstrong, Henry, *82,* 83
Army (team), 36, 40, 41
Art Ross Trophy, 93
Ashe, Arthur, 144, *145*
association football,
see soccer
Athletic Sports Union, 127
Australia, 132, 134, 142,
143, 144, 147, 148, 150,
151, 152

B

Babe Ruth League, 6
Bagby, Jim (Jr.), 10
Baltimore Colts, 47, 48, 49
Baltimore Orioles, 12, 20
Banks, Dave, 66
"Barbados Demon,"
see Walcott, Joe

Barry, Jimmy, 88
Barry, Pete, 66
Baseball, 5-30, 51
Baseball Museum, 5
Basilio, Carmen, *84*
Basketball, 53-70
batting, 6, 7, 9, 10, 11, 12,
15, 16, 23, 24, 26, 29, 30
Battling Nelson, 81, 82, 86
Bauer sisters, 126
Baugh, Sammy, 46
Baylor, Elgin, 63, *64*
Beamon, Bob, *128*
Beard, Ralph, 57
Beckman, Johnnie, 66
Beliveau, Jean, 95
Belkin, Mike, 148
Berg, Patty, 126
Berra, Yogi, 13, 23, *26*
Berry, Raymond, 47, 48
Bevans, Floyd, 23
"Big Dipper,"
see Chamberlain, Wilt
"Big O,"
see Robertson, Oscar
Blaik, Earl ("Red"), 46
Blake, Hector ("Toe"),
95, 98
Blanchard, Felix ("Doc"),
37, *41*
Blanda, George, 52
Blankers-Koen, Francina
("Fanny"), 140
"blitz," 35
blocking, 45
Blood, Ernie, 68
Bloomfield Rams, 47
"Boilermaker,"
see Jeffries, James J.
Borgman, Benny, 66
Boros, Julius, 118
Borotra, Jean, 146
Boston Bruins, 91, 94,
95, 96
Boston Celtics, 60, 61, 62,
64, 66
Boston, Ralph, 128, 137
Boston Red Sox, 11, 17,
18, 24
Boucher, Frank, 98
Bowen, Andy, 87
Bowl games,
see specific names
Boxing, 71-88
Bradley, Bill, 44
Bradley University, 57
Bragg, Don, 135
Branca, Ralph, 27

Brecheen, Harry
("The Cat"), 24
British Amateur Golf
Tournament, 114, 126
British Open Golf
Tournament, 106, 109,
112, 114, 115, 118, 119,
123, 124
"Broadway Joe,"
see Namath, Joe
Bromwich, Jack, 148, 151
"Bronko," *see* Nagurski,
Bronko
"Bronx Bombers,"
see New York Yankees
Brooker, Tommy, 52
Brooklyn Dodgers, 12, 18,
22, 23, 26, 27
Broughton, Jack, 72
"Brown Bomber,"
see Louis, Joe
Brown, C. S. (Mrs.), 108
Brown, Jimmy, 37, *38*
Brown, Paul, 50
Brown, William
("Rookey"), 68
Brugge, Harry, 66
Brugnon, Jacques, 146
Brumel, Valery, 136, *137*
Budge, Don, *142,* 143,
148, 151, 154
Buffalo Bills, 50
Bunning, Jim, 17, 23
Burdette, Lew, 24
Burke, Jack, 87

C

Calder, Frank, 96
California, University of
(U.C.L.A.), 39, 56, 57,
58, 69
Campbell, Clarence S.,
92, 93, 98
Campbell, Milt, 139
Campbell, Willie, 107
Canadian Amateur
Hockey Association, 89
Canadian National
Exhibition, 90
Canton Bulldogs, 52
Canzoneri, Tony, 82, 83
Carner, Jo Anne
Gunderson, 125
Carr, Joe, 52
Cartwright, Alexander, *7*
Casey, Hugh, 23
Casper, Billy, 124
"Catapult-shoe," 136

catchers, 8, 26
Cattarinich, Joe, 97
Celtics, 66.
See also Boston Celtics
Chace, Malcolm G., 103
Chadwick, Bill, *92,*
101, 103
Chamberlain, Wilt,
58, 60, 61, 62
Cherry Hills (golf course),
121
Chicago Bears, 43
Chicago Black Hawks, 91,
92, 94, 95, 98, 100
Chicago Cardinals, 52
Chicago Cubs, 10, 15, 18
Chicago Tribune, 28
Chicago White Sox, 12, 24
Cincinnati, University of,
57, 62
Cincinnati Royals, 62
City College of New York,
57, 66
Clarke, Ron, 134
Clarkson, John, 17
Clay, Cassius,
See Ali, Muhammed
Cleveland Browns, 50
Cleveland Indians
(baseball team), 12, 18
Cleveland Indians
(football team), 52
Clifton, Nat
("Sweetwater"), 59
"Clown Prince of
Baseball,"
see Schacht, Al
"Clown Prince of
Basketball," *see* Tatum,
Reece ("Goose")
coaches, 43, 44, 47, 49, 52,
56, 57, 58, 66, 68, 69,
98, 143, 144
Cobb, Ty, 9, 10, *14,* 15
Cochet, Henri, 146
Colavito, Rocky, 12
Collins, Eddie, 14, 15
Colorado, University of,
43, 44
Columbia University, 33
Conn Smythe Trophy, 99
Cook, Bill, 98
Cook, Bun, 98
Coombs, Jack, 24
Cooper, Don, 135
Cooperstown, N. Y., 5
Corbett, James J., 74, *75*
Cotton Bowl, 44

Coubertin, Pierre de, 127
court tennis, 141
Coveleski, Stanley, 24
Cravath, Jeff, 43
Creighton, J. G. A., 90
cricket, 5
Cronin, Joe, 29
Crosetti, Frank, 65
Crowley, Jim, *40*
Cruikshank, Bobby, 114
Cunningham, Glenn, 131, *132*

D

Dallas Cowboys, 46
Dallas Texans, 52
Dandurand, Leo, 97
Dark, Alvin, 27
Davidson, Ben, *48*
Davis Cup, 144, 147, 149, 150, 152, 154
Davis, Dwight, 144
Davis, Glenn, 37, *41*
Dawson, Len, 52
Dayton Triangles, 52
decathlon, 45, 139
Decatur Staleys, 52
Dehnert, "Dutch," 66
Delahanty, Ed, 12
Delvechio, Alex, 95
DeMatha High School, 68
Dempsey, Jack, *76, 77, 79,* 80, 81, 84, *85,* 88
DePaul University, 58
Detroit Cougars, 91
Detroit Lions, 44
Detroit Red Wings, 91, 92, 94, 96
Detroit Tigers, 10, 17, 18, 25
Dickey, Bill, 29
Didrikson, Mildred ("Babe"), *see* Zaharias, Mildred ("Babe") Didrikson
Dillard, Harrison, 131
DiMaggio, Joe, 10, *13,* 65
Dinneen, Bill, 24
Dipley, Walter, 83
Disney, Walt, 67
Doeg, Johnny, 151
Donovan, Arthur, 88
Dorais, Charlie ("Gus"), 36
Doubleday, Abner, *5,* 31
Dressen, Chuck, 27
dribbling, 54, 63, 66, 68
Drysdale, Cliff, 148

Drysdale, Don, *21,* 30
Dumas, Charles, 136
Dunn, Willie, 107
Durelle, Yvonne, *86*
Durnan, Bill, 97
Durocher, Leo, 26

E

Ebbets Field, 40
Edwards, Bruce, 23
eligible receiver, 36
Elliott, Herb, 132
Ellis, William, 32
Emerson, Roy, 151
ERA's, 19, 20, 25
Erickson, Keith, *61*
Erne, Frank, 81
Esposito, Phil, 94, 95
Evans, Lee, 129
even defense, 34
Ewbank, Weeb, 47

F

Faber, Urban, 24
Feathers, Beattie, 43
Federation Cup, 152
Feller, Robert, *18,* 19, 20, 21
Ferguson, Norm, 95
Figg, James, 72
fighting, *see* boxing
Firpo, Luis Angel, 77, *85*
Fitzsimmons, Bob, *71,* 74, 83
Fleischer, Nat, 76
Foley, Larry, 88
football, 31-52
Foote, Arthur E., 103
Ford, Whitey, 24, *25,* 26
Fordham University, 46, 47
Forest Hills Stadium, 147, 154
forward pass, 36, 37, 44, 45
"Four Horsemen," *40*
Fox, Joseph Mickle, 106, 107
Foxburg Golf Club, 107
Foxx, Jimmy, 11, 15, 16, 29
Fraser, Neale, 143, 144, 151
Fresh Meadow Country Club, 111, 115
Furillo, Carl, 23

G

Gadsby, Bill, 95
Gaines, Joseph, *see* Gans, Joe
Galvin, James, 17
Gans, Joe, 81, 83
Garcia, Ceferino, 83
Gehrig, Lou, 11, 12, *13,* 15, 29
Gehringer, Charlie, 29
"Gentleman Jim," *see* Corbett, James J.
Geoffrion, Bernie ("Boom-Boom"), 95
"Georgia Peach," *see* Cobb, Ty
Georgia Tech, 39
Gibson, Bob, 20, 24, *25*
Gifford, Frank, 47
Giles, H. A., 32
Gionfriddo, Al, 23
Globetrotters, *see* Harlem Globetrotters
gloves, 6, 74
"Golden Bear," *see* Nicklaus, Jack
Golden Bears, 39
Goldman, Charlie, 79
Golf, 105-126
Gomez, Lefty, 29
Gonzales, Richard ("Pancho"), 142, 147, 154, *155*
Goodrich, Gail, 58
Goss, Joe, 73
Graebner, Carole, 152
Graebner, Clark, 144
Graham, Otto, 46, *50*
grand slam
    golf, 114, 122, 124
    tennis, 143
Grange, Harold ("Red"), 37, 41, *42,* 44, 65
Grant, Bryon ("Bitsy"), *147*
Grant, Danny, 95
Greb, Harry, *79,* 83, 84
Green Bay Packers, 46
Greenberg, Hank, 15, 16
Grider, Josh, 68
Grove, Robert Moses ("Lefty"), 17, 20, 24
Groza, Alex, *57*
Guldahl, Ralph, 119
gutta-percha ball, 106

H

Haddix, Harvey, 19
Hagan, Cliff, 60
Hagen, Walter, 109, *111,* 112, 114, 119, 120
Hagg, Gunder, 134
Haggerty, George, 66
Hall, Glenn, 97
Hall of Fame
    baseball, 5, 7, 10
    hockey, 89, 90, 92
    sports, 90
    tennis, 150
Hamilton, Billy, 15
Hanson, Beverly, 126
Harlem Globetrotters, 25, *67,* 68
Harmon, Tommy, *35,* 37
Harpaston, 32
Harris, Bucky, 13, 23
Hart, Cecil, 92
Hart, David A., 92
Hart Memorial Trophy, 92, 94, 99
Hartung, Clint, 27
Harvey, Doug, 96, *97*
Havlin, Jack, 86
Hayes, Bob, *130*
Hayes, Elvin, 58
Haynes, Abner, 52
Haynes, Marques, 68
Hays, Ralph, 52
Hazzard, Walt, 58
heavyweights, 74, 75, 76, 77, 78, 79, 80, 81, 83, 84, *85,* 86, 88
Heffelfinger, "Pudge," 51
Heilmann, Harry, 10
Heldman, Julie, 152
Hemery, Dave, 129
Hennessey, John, 151
Herman, Billie, 29
Heston, Willie, 37
Hickey, Eddie, 69
Hines, Jim, 128
Hoad, Lew, 143, 144, 151
hockey, 89-104
Hodge, Ken, 95
Hodges, Gil, 12
Hogan, Ben, 105, 108, 116, *117,* 118, 119, 120, 124
Hogan, Valerie, 117
hole in one, 124
Hollett, Flash, 94
Holloman, Alva ("Bobo"), 19

Holman, Nat, 57, 66
Homans, Gene, 114
home runs, 6, 8, 9, 11, 12, 15, 16, 22, 24, 26, 27, 29, 30
"Hondo Hurricane," *see* Hartung, Clint
Hopman, Harry, 143, 144, 150
Houk, Ralph, 13
Houston Astrodome, 58, 61
Houston Oilers, 52
Hornsby, Rogers, 10, 11, *13*
Howe, Gordie, 92, 94, 95, 98, 99, *100*
Hoy, Bill ("Dummy'"), 8
Hubbell, Carl, *28*, 29
Huggins, Miller, 13
Hull, Robert Marvin ("Bobby"), 92, 94, 96, 100, 101, 102
"Human Windmill," *see* Greb, Harry
Hunnewell, Hollis, 141
Hunter, Jim ("Catfish"), 23, 30
Hyer, Jacob, 72
Hyer, Tom, 72

I

Iba, Henry, 56
Idaho, College of, 63
Illinois, University of, 41, *42*
in-bounds markers, 35
Indiana University, 139
International Amateur Athletic Federation, 136, 137
International Lawn Tennis Federation, 143
Inwood Country Club, 113
Irvin, Monte, 27

J

Jackson, Joe, 10
Jacobs, Helen, *145*
James II, 105
James IV, 105
James V, 105
Jameson, Betty, 126
Jeffries, James J., *71*, 74, *75*, 78, 79
Jerome, Harry, 130
Johnson, Jack, 74, 75, *76*, 81, 83
Johnson, James, 130

Johnson, Rafer, 139
Johnson, Walter, 17, 20, 21
Johnston, Billy, 146
Jones, Bobby, 108, 112, *113*, 114, 118, 119, 122
Jones, Hayes, 131
Jorgensen, Spider, 23
Joss, Adrian, 23
Jucker, Ed, 57
jump shot, 65, 66

K

Kane, Jim, 66
Kansas, University of, 58, 61
Keefe, Jim, 17
Keeler, Wee Willie, 10
Keino, Kipchoge, 129
Keltner, Ken, 10
Kennedy, John F., 44
Kentucky University, 57
Keogan, George, 68, 69
Ketchell, Stanley, 83
Killebrew, Harmon, 12
Kilroy, Mathew, 21
Kiner, Ralph, 16, 30
King, Billie Jean (Mrs.), 152
King of Sweden, 45
Kingston Athletics, 90
Kingston Hockey Club, 90
Klein, Chuck, 11, 12
Knickerbocker Baseball Club, 7
knockdowns, 83, 85, 86, 87
knockouts, 72, 77, 78, 79, 80, 81, 82, 83, 85, 86, 87
Kooyong Stadium, 147
Koufax, Sandy, *18*, 21, 23, 24, 25
Kraft, Jack, 69
Kramer, Jack, 142, *151*, 154
Kretlow, Lou, 124
Kurland, Bob, 56
Kuznetsov, Vasily, 139

L

Lach, Elmer, 95
Lacoste, Rene, 146
Lady Byng Trophy, 98
Lajoie, Napoleon, 10, 14
Lapchick, Joe, 66
Larsen, Don, *22*
Lash, Don, *134*
Lavagetto, Harry ("Cookie"), 23

Laver, Don, *142*, 143, 144
Layden, Elmer, *40*
LayoMayo, Joaquin, 147
Laz, Don, 135
Lazzeri, Tony, 20, 65
Leahy, Frank, 46
Lehigh-Lafayette game, *31*
Lenglen, Suzanne, 146, *153*
Lenoir, Billy, 148
Leonard, Benny, 82, 83
Leonard, Chris, 66
Letourneau, Louis, 97
Levinsky, "Kingfish," 77
light heavyweights, 74, 84, 86
Lindgren, Gerry, 134
Lindsay, John, 66
Lindsay, Ted, 95
Liston, Sonny, *80*
Little League Baseball, 6
Lockman, Whitey, 27
Loes, Billy, 12
Lom, Benny, 39
Lombardi, Vince, 46, *47*, 50
"long count," 77, 79
Long, Dallas, 139
Lord Kilcoursie, 90, 91
Lord Stanley, 90, 91
Los Angeles Dodgers, 21
Los Angeles Kings, 91
Los Angeles Lakers, 58, 61, 63, 64
Lott, George, 151
Louis, Joe, 77, *78*, 79, 81, 88
Lovellette, Clyde, 60
Lowe, Robert, 12
Lucas, Jerry, 58, 62
Luckman, Sid, 46
Luisetti, Angelo Enrico ("Hank"), *65*
Lutz, Robert, 144

M

"M & M boys," 16
MacDonald, C. B., 107
Mack, Connie, 51
Madison Square Garden, 51, 56, 64, 65, 66
Maglie, Sal, 22
Mahovlich, Frank, *95*, 96
Mako, Gene, 151
Malone, Joe, 94
man-for-man defense, 35, 68, 69, 70

"Manassa Mauler," *see* Dempsey, Jack
Mantle, Mickey, 12, *16*, 22
Manush, Heinie, 29
Marchetti, Gino, 47
Marciano, Rocky, 79, *80*, 81, 86, 88
Maris, Roger, *16*
Massillon Tigers, 52
Masters Golf Tournament, 115, 116, 118, 119, 123, 124
Mathewson, Christy, 17, 24, 51
Mathias, Bob, 135
Matson, Randy, 138, 139
Maxim, Joey, 84, 86
Mays, Willie, 12, 14, 15, 16, 24, 27, *28*, 29
McAuliffe, Jack, 88
McCann, Brendan, 63
McCarthy, Joe, 13
McDermott, Johnny, 111
McGill University, 90
McGrath, Vivian, 148
McGregor, Ken, 144
McLain, Denny, 25
McManus, Jim, 148
McQuinn, George, 23
Meadowbrook Club, 108
Medwick, Joe, 11
Meehan, "Stretch," 66
Merion Cricket Club, 114
Metcalfe, Ralph, 130
Meyers, Ray, 58
Michigan, University of, 35
"Michigan Assassin," 83
Mikan, George, 58, *59*, 60
Mikita, Stan, 92, 94, 95, 98
Miller, Don, *40*
Mills, Billy, 134
Milwaukee Braves, 12, 19, 24
Minneapolis Lakers, 58, 59
Minnesota, University of, 43
Minnesota North Stars, 91
Miracle Hills Golf Club, 124
Mitchell, Dale, 22
Mitera, Robert, 124
Mize, Johnny, 16
Montreal Canadiens, 91, 92, 94, 95, 97, 98, 100, 101
Montreal Wanderers, 91

Moody, Helen Wills, *141,* 145, 146, 153
Moore, Archie, 74, *86*
Moore, Lenny, 47
Morenz, Howie, 92
Morris, Tom, 106
"Mr. Inside," *41*
"Mr. Outside," *41*
Mueller, "Chief," 66
Mueller, Don ("Mandrake,") 27
Mullaney, Joe, 69
Mulloy, Gardner, *149,* 151
Murphy, Ron, *95*
Musial, Stan, *14,* 15, 28
Mutscheller, Jim, 48
Myrha, Steve, 48

N

Nagurski, Bronko, *42,* 43
Naismith, James A., *53, 54, 55*
Namath, Joe, 31, 45, 46, 47, *48,* 49, 50, 53
National Baseball League, 10, 11, 12, 13, 14, 15, 18, 20, 23, 27, 28, 29, 30
National Basketball Association, 60, 61, 62, 64
National Boxing Association, 87
National Collegiate Athletic Association, 56, 57, 58, 62, 66
National Football League, 43, 44, 50, 51, 130
National Hockey Association, 91
National Hockey League, 90, 91, 92, 93, 94, 96, 97, 101, 103, 104
National Invitation Tournament, 57, 63, 66
Navy (team), 41
Neider, Bill, 139
Nelson, Byron, 116, 126
Nelson, Cordner, 132
Nevers, Ernie, 37
New York Americans, 91
"New York Game," 6
New York Giants (baseball team), 10, 11, 13, 14, 18, 20, 24, 26, 27
New York Giants (football team), 46, 47, 48

New York Jets, 49
New York Knickerbockers, 59, 60, 66
New York Mets, 17, 18
New York Nine, 7
New York Rangers, 91, 98
New York Yankees, 12, *13,* 15, 16, 18, 20, 22, 23, 24, 25, 26, 65
New Zealand, 127
Newcombe, Don, 26, 27
Nichols, Charles, 17
Nicklaus, Jack, *122,* 123, 124
Nighbor, Frank, 92
Norris, James, 96
Notre Dame, University of, 36, 37, 40, 41, 51, 58, 68
Nurmi, Paavo, 134

O

Oakland Raiders, 48
Oakland Seals, 91
O'Brien, Parry, *138, 139*
o'cat, 6
odd defense, 34
Ohio State University, 58
Okker, Tom, 145
Oklahoma A. & M., 56
Oklahoma State University, 56
Oliver, Ed ("Porky"), 116
Olympics, 45, 55, 103, 126, 127, 128, 129, 131, 137, 139
Orr, Bobby, 94, *95,* 96
Ott, Mel, 11
Ouimet, Francis, *105,* 109, 110, 111, 112, 113
Owens, Jesse, 128, *129,* 130, 131

P

Packers, *see* Green Bay Packers
Palmer, Arnold, 105, 120, *121,* 123, 124
Palmer, John ("Bud"), 66
Papke, Bill, 83
Park, Willie (Sr.), 106
Patterson, Floyd, 88
Peacock, Eulace, 130
pennants, 13
Pennel, John, 135
Pennsylvania, University of, 42

perfect game(s), 22, 23, 30
Perry, Fred, 143
Pettit, Bob, 60
Philadelphia Athletics, 11, 12, 24
Philadelphia Flyers, 91
Philadelphia Phils, 17, 18
Phillippe, Deacon, 24
Pilote, Pierre, 95, 96
Pinelli, Babe, 22
pitchers, 7, 8, 9, 10, 16, 17, 18, 19, 20, 21, 22, 23, 24, 25, 26, 27, 28, 29, 30
Pittsburgh Penguins, 91
Pittsburgh Pirates, 19
Pittsburgh Steelers, 44, 46
Plank, Eddie, 17
Plante, Jacques, *89, 97,* 100, *104*
Player, Gary, 124
pole-vaulting, 135, 136
Polo Grounds, 26, 27, 40
"Pottowotomie Giant," *see* Willard, Jess
Power Memorial High School, 68
Prestwick Club, 106
Prince of Wales Trophy, 93, 98
Princeton University, 32, 36
Professional Golfers' Association, 112, 115, 116, 119, 123, 124
Pryor, Billy, 88
Purdue University, 56

Q

Queen's University, 90

R

Radbourne, Charles, 17
Ratterman, George, 50
Rawlins, Horace, 107
Rawls, Betsy, 126
Ray, Ted, *105,* 108, 109, 110, 111
RBI's, 10, 11, 12
Reagan, Ronald, 20
"red dog," *see* "blitz"
Reese, Pee Wee, 22
referees, 77, 82, 85, 87, 88, 101, 103
Reich, Ernie, 66
Reid, John, 107
Reiser, Pete, 15, 23

Reynolds, Allie, 18
Rhodes scholar, 44
Rice, Grantland, 40
Rice University, 43, 44
Richard, Maurice ("Rocket"), *89, 95,* 100, 101, *102*
Richards, Bob, 135
Richards, Vinnie, 146, 151
Richey, Cliff, *152*
Richey, Nancy, *152*
Riegels, "Wrong Way," *39*
Ripley, Elmer, 66
Roberts, R. J., 53
Robertson, C. C., 23
Robertson, Oscar, 58, *62*
Robinson, Ermer, 68
Robinson, Frank, 12
Robinson, Sugar Ray, *84,* 85
Roche, Tony, 143
Rockne, Knute, 36, *37,* 51
Rose Bowl, *33,* 39
Rosewall, Ken, 143, 144, 147, 151
Ross, Art, 93, 94, 99
Ross, Barney, 82, 83
rounders, 6
Royal Military College, 90
Rudolph, Wilma, 131
Ruel, Claude, 98
Rugby, 32
rules, 7, 8, 55, 56, 72
Rupp, Adolph, 57
Russell, Bill, 57, 58, 59, 60, *61,* 62, 63
Rutgers University, 32
Ruth, George Herman ("Babe"), 9, *11,* 15, 16, 19, 24, 29, 65, 101
Ryan, Paddy, 73
Ryun, James ("Jim"), *127,* 131, 132

S

Sailors, Kenny, 65
San Francisco, University of, 57
San Francisco Giants, 12
San Romani, Archie, 131, 132
Sands, C. E., 107
Saneyev, Viktor, 129
Santa Clara, 57
Santee, Wes, 131, 132
Saperstein, Abe, 67
Sarazan, Gene, *115,* 119, 124

Sayers, Gale, 37, *38*, 130
Sayers, Rogers, 130
Schacht, Al, 20
Schmeling, Max, *78*
Schoendienst, Red, 30
Schroeder, Ted, 151
Schud, Bob, 134
Schupp, Ferd, 20
scoring 8, *9*, 63, 65, 87, 94 150
screwball, 28
Seattle University, 63
Sedgman, Frank, 143, 144, *145*, 151
Seerey, Pat, 12
Segura, Pancho, 148
Sesqui-Centennial Stadium, 88
"Seven Blocks of Granite," 46, 47
Shore, Eddie, *92*
Shore, Ernie, 19, 23
Shotten, Burt, 23
Shute, Denny, 116
Simmons, Al, 12, 29
Simpson, O. J., 37-38
single-wing, 32
Sisler, George, 10
Smith, Al, 10
Smith, Margaret, 150, 152
Smith, Sherry, 24
Smith, Stan, 144
Smith, Tommie, 128
Smith, Walker, *see* Robinson, Sugar Ray
Smythe, Conn, 99
Snead, Sam, 116, *118*, 119, 126
Snell, Peter, *127*, 132, *133*
soccer, 32, 54
softball, 6
Soldiers Field, 88
Souchak, Big Mike, 121
Southwest Conference, 44
Spahn, Warren, *17*
Speaker, Tris, 14
Spears, "Doc," 43
Speiser, E. A., 71
Spikes, Jack, 52
Springfield College, 53, 55
St. Andrews Golf Club, 107
St. Louis Blues, 91, 97
St. Louis Cardinals, 11, 20, 24, 30
St. Louis Hawks, 60, 64
St. Louis University, 69
Stallard, Tracy, 16

Stanford University, 33, 65
Stanky, Eddie, 23
Stanley Cup, *89*, 90, 99, 101
Stapleton, Pat, 95
Starr, Bart, 46, 50
"Staten Island Scot," *see* Thomson, Bobby
Stengel, Casey, 13
Stepanov, Yuri, 136
stickball, 6
Stoefen, Les, 151
stolen bases, 15, 29
Stovey, Harry, 15
Stram, Hank, 52
Stuhldreher, Harry, *40*
Sugar Bowl, 31
Suggs, Louise, 126
Sullivan, John L., *73*, 74
Sullivan, Mike ("Twin"), 83
Super Bowl, 31, 49
Supreme Court, 43, 44

T
"T" formations, 32, 33, 34
Talbert, Billy, *149*, 151
Tatum, Reece ("Goose"), *67*
Tendler, Lew, 82
tennis, 141-154
Ter-Ovanesyan, Igor, 128, 137
Terry, Bill, 10, 11
Thayer, Nathaniel, 141
Thomas, John, *136*, 137
Thomson, Bobby, 26, *27*
Thorpe, Jim, 37, *44*, 45, 51, 52
Tilden, Bill, *142*, 146, 148, 151, 154
Tolar, Charlie, 52
Tolley, Cyril, 114
Toney, Fred, 19
Toronto Arenas, 91
Toronto Maple Leafs, 91, 99
"Touchdown Twins," 41
touchdowns, 36, 37, 38, 41, 42, 44
"Town Ball," 6
track and field, 126, 127-140
Track and Field News, 132
Trucks, Virgil, 18
Tunney, Gene, 77, 78, *79*, 83, 88

U
Uclans, *see* California, University of
Uelses, John, 135
Ullman, Norm, 95
umpires, 8, 19, 20, 22
Union of Soviet Socialist Republics, 137, 139
Unitas, Johnny, 46, *47*, 48, 49, 50
United States Golf Association, 107, 108
United States Lawn Tennis Association, 150
United States National Amateur Tournament, 112, 113, 114, 120, 122, 123, 126
United States Open Golf Championship, 105, 107, 108, 109, 111, 112, 113, 114, 115, 116, 118, 119, 121, 122, 123, 124

V
Van Alan Simplified Scoring System, 150
Van Brocklin, Norm, 46
Vander Meer, Johnny, *17*, 18
Vardon, Harry, *105*, 108, 109, 110, 111, 126
Vaughn, Jim, 19
Vebina, Georges, 97
Venturi, Ken, 120
Vernon, Mickey, 28
Vezina Trophy, 97
Vines, Ellsworth, 142, 154, *155*

W
Waddell, Rube, 21
Wagner, Honus, 9, 14
Walcott, Joe, 75, 81, 88
Walker, Mickey, 84
Waner, Paul, 14
Ward, Arch, 28, 29
Warmerdam, Cornelius, 134, *135*
Warner, Pop, 51
Warren, Tommy, 86
Washington Senators, 17, 18
Waterfield, Bob, 46
Welch, Michael, 17
West, Jerry, 63, *64*
West Point, 36, 46
West Virginia Mountaineers, 63

Western Open Golf Championship, 116
Westmount Arena, 91
Wethered, Joyce, 126
Wethered, Roger, 114
Wheeler, Sam, 68
White, Byron ("Whizzer"), 43, *44*
White, G. Harris, 21
Whitworth, Kathy, 125
Wightman Cup, 148
Wilhelm, Hoyt, 20
Willard, Jess, 76, 77
Williams, Christy, 86
Williams, R. Norris, 146
Williams, Ted, 10, *11*, 28, 30
Wills, Helen, *see* Moody, Helen Wills
Wills, Maury, 15
Wilson, Clarence, 68
Wilson, Louis Robert ("Hack"), *14*, 15, 16
"Wilt the Stilt," *see* Chamberlain, Wilt
Wimbledon Open Title, 143, 147, 153, 154
Wingfield, Walter, 141
Wolverines, 41, 42, 69
Woman Athlete of the Year, 125
Wood, Craig, 115, 116
Wood, Smokey Joe, 24
Wooden, John, 58
Woolpert, Phil, 57
World Series, 13, 20, 22, 23, 24, 25, 26
Worsham, Lew, 119
Wright, Mickey, *125*
Wynn, Early, 17, 28

Y
Yale University, 36, 51
Yang, C. K., 139
Yankee Stadium, 22
Yastrzemski, Carl, 12
Young, Denton ("Cy"), *17*, 18, 23

Z
Zachary, Tom, *11*
Zaharias, Mildred ("Babe") Didrikson, *125*, 126, 139, *140*
Zale, Tony, 88
Zatopek, Emil, 134
Zimmerman, Heinie, 10
zone defense, 35, 68, 69, *70*